CHILT WALKS

HERTFORDSHIRE, BEDFORDSHIRE
& NORTH BUCKINGHAMSHIRE

Nick Moon

This book is one of a series of three which provide a comprehensive coverage of walks throughout the whole of the Chiltern area (as defined by the Chiltern Society). The walks included vary in length from 2.1 to 11.4 miles, but are mainly in the 5- to 7-mile range popular for half-day walks, although suggestions of possible combinations of walks are given for those preferring a full day's walk.

Each walk gives details of nearby places of interest and is accompanied by a specially drawn map of the route which also indicates local pubs and a skeleton road network.

The author, Nick Moon, has lived in or regularly visited the Chilterns all his life and has, for 20 years, been an active member of the Chiltern Society's Rights of Way Group, which seeks to protect and improve the area's footpath and bridleway network. Thanks to the help and encouragement of the late Don Gresswell MBE, he was introduced to the writing of books of walks and has since written or contributed to a number of publications in this field.

The
Chiltern
Society

OTHER PUBLICATIONS BY NICK MOON

Chiltern Walks Trilogy

Chiltern Walks 1 :   Hertfordshire, Bedfordshire and
                       North Buckinghamshire : Book Castle 1993
Chiltern Walks 2 :   Buckinghamshire : Book Castle
                       new edition 1993
Chiltern Walks 3 :   Oxfordshire and West Buckinghamshire :
                       Book Castle 1992

Complete Books

Walks for Motorists: Chilterns (Southern Area): Frederick Warne 1979
Walks for Motorists: Chilterns (Northern Area): Frederick Warne 1979
Walks in the Hertfordshire Chilterns: Shire 1986

Contributions

Chiltern Society Footpath Maps: a number of walk descriptions –
                                  also all map checking since c.1975
Walks in the Countryside round London: W. Foulsham & Co Ltd. 1985
Walker's Britain: Pan 1982
Walker's Britain II: Pan 1986

First published April 1993
by The Book Castle
12 Church Street, Dunstable, Bedfordshire

© Nick Moon, 1993

Computer Typeset by Keyword, Aldbury, Herts
Printed in Great Britain by Alden Press, Oxford

ISBN 1 871199 51 4

All rights reserved

Contents

CHILTERN WALKS: HERTFORDSHIRE, BEDFORDSHIRE & NORTH BUCKINGHAMSHIRE : LIST OF WALKS

POSSIBLE LONGER WALKS PRODUCED BY COMBINING WALKS DESCRIBED IN THE BOOK

Walks	Miles	Km	Walks	Miles	Km
2A + 3	13.2	21.2	14A + 15	16.9	27.2
2A + 3 + 4A	19.7	31.7	14C + 15	13.1	21.0
2A + 4A	13.4	21.6	17 + 18A	13.0	21.0
2A + 4A + 5	20.9	33.6	19 + 20	14.6	23.5
2B + 3	12.1	19.4	21A + 22	15.3	24.7
2B + 3 + 4B	18.0	29.0	23 + 24	13.4	21.5
2B + 4B	11.7	18.9	23 + 24 + 25	21.5	34.7
2B + 4B + 5	19.2	30.9	23 + 24 + 26A	21.7	34.9
4A + 5	14.0	22.5	23 + 24 + 26B	15.3	24.7
4B + 5	13.4	21.6	23 + 25	15.0	24.2
7A + 8	16.7	26.9	23 + 25 + 26A	20.2 or 23.6	32.6 or 38.0
7A + 14A	16.9	27.2	23 + 25 + 26B	17.3	27.8
7A + 14B	14.3	23.0	24 + 25 + 26B	17.4	28.1
7B+ 8	11.2	17.9	25 + 26A	13.1 or 16.4	21.0 or 26.4
7C + 14A	14.2	22.8	25 + 26B	10.1	16.2
7C + 14B	11.6	18.6	26A + 27	15.7	25.2
9 + 12A	13.6	22.0	26A + 28	16.9	27.3
9 + 12A + 13	21.5	34.5	26C + 27	13.7	22.1
9 + 12B	12.7	20.5	26C + 27 + 28	21.8	35.1
9 + 12B + 13	20.6	33.1	26C + 28	15.0	24.1
9 + 13	14.8	23.8	27 + 28	14.6	23.5
13 + 17	12.5	20.1	27 + 28 + 29	21.8	35.2
13 + 17 + 18A	19.3	31.0	28 + 29	14.6	23.6

Cover Photograph: View from Highpark Wood looking across Water End towards Gaddesden Place. (Walk 7). © Nick Moon.

Introduction

This book of walks is one of three covering the whole of the Chilterns from the Goring Gap on the River Thames to the Hitchin Gap in North Hertfordshire. The area covered by this volume includes the whole of the Hertfordshire and Bedfordshire Chilterns as well as the detached part of the Buckinghamshire Chilterns north of Tring. From a geographical point of view the county boundaries in this area have no logical basis and in practice the area covered by this book, which offers the walker a great variety of attractive countryside to explore, is divided into two distinct parts both by its natural geography and the influence of man, the dividing line being the M1 and Luton and Dunstable conurbation. To the southwest of this line the hills are traversed by the River Colne and its tributaries, the Ver, Gade, Bulbourne and Chess, which flow southwards to join the Thames in Staines to the west of London, whereas to the northeast of it, the River Lea which rises in Luton and its tributary, the Mimram flow southeastwards to join the Thames in East London and in the extreme northeast corner, the Hiz and its tributaries, the Oughton and the Purwell, flow northwards into the Ouse.

Within this area to the north and east of Luton, the escarpment, here known as the Barton Hills, includes some of the finest and yet least known downland in the Chilterns, while the interior is dominated by Lilley Bottom, a wide valley resembling Hampden Bottom in Bucks, which becomes the Mimram valley above Whitwell. The hills to the northeast of this valley traversed by a maze of narrow lanes are quiet and well-wooded and so are most inviting for the walker to explore. To the southwest a more open ridge gradually giving way to the gentle rolling hills of Central Hertfordshire separates Lilley Bottom from Luton and the Lea valley.

South of the Luton conurbation the first ridge separating the Lea and Ver valleys and climbing to the lofty heights of Blow's Down is generally open in nature and has suffered somewhat from insensitive development. The next ridge, however, between the Ver and Gade valleys dropping gently from the mighty Dunstable Downs to Hemel Hempstead and the M1, and the Gade valley above Hemel have been largely spared the scourge of modern development and with their scattering of woods and remote rural atmosphere offer an expanse of fine walking country. Between the Gade and Bulbourne valleys is a ridge dominated by the Ashridge Estate which rises to the Ivinghoe Hills and with its mixture of copious woodland, picturesque villages and lofty downs is probably the most popular walking area in this book. South of the Bulbourne valley, where the Grand Union Canal towpath and Tring Reservoirs provide pleasant waterside walks, is a range of hills straddled by the Bucks. boundary and the Chess valley, probably the most attractive valley in the northern Chilterns, while finally to the south of Rickmansworth the Colne valley and hills on the former Middlesex border offer surprisingly rural walks with fine views within twenty miles of Central London.

The majority of walks included in this book are in the 5–7 mile range which is justifiably popular for half-day walks, but, for the less energetic or for short winter afternoons, a few shorter versions are indicated in the text, while others can be devised with the assistance of a map. In addition, a number of walks in the 7–11 mile range are included for those preferring a leisurely day's walk or for longer spring and summer afternoons, while a list of possible combinations of walks is provided for those favouring a full day's walk of up to 23 miles.

All the walks described here follow public rights of way, use recognised permissive paths or cross public open space. As the majority of walks cross land used for economic purposes such as agriculture, forestry or the rearing of game, walkers are urged to follow the Country Code at all times:

- Guard against all risk of fire
- Fasten all gates
- Keep dogs under proper control
- Keep to the paths across farmland
- Avoid damaging fences, hedges and walls
- Leave no litter – take it home
- Safeguard water supplies
- Protect wild life, wild plants and trees
- Go carefully on country roads on the right-hand side facing oncoming traffic
- Respect the life of the countryside

Observing these rules helps prevent financial loss to landowners and damage to the environment, as well as the all-too-frequent and sometimes justified bad feeling towards walkers in the countryside.

While it is hoped that the special maps provided with each walk will assist the user to complete the walks without going astray and skeleton details of the surrounding road network are given to enable walkers to shorten the routes in emergency, it is always advisable to take an Ordnance Survey or Chiltern Society map with you to enable you to shorten or otherwise vary the routes without using roads or get your bearings if you do become seriously lost. Details of the appropriate maps are given in the introductory information of each walk.

6

As for other equipment, readers are advised that some mud will normally be encountered on most walks particularly in woodland except in the driest weather. However proper walking boots are to be recommended at all times as, even when there are no mud problems, hard ruts or rough surfaces make the protection given by boots to the ankles desirable. In addition, the nature of the countryside makes many Chiltern paths prone to overgrowth, particularly in summer. To avoid resultant discomfort, protective clothing is advisable, especially where specific warnings are given.

Some of the walks may be familiar to readers as they were previously published in 'Walks in the Hertfordshire Chilterns' or 'Walks for Motorists : Chilterns (Northern Area)' which are now out of print, but more than half are completely new or have been radically altered, while all of the old walks have been rechecked and brought up to date. In addition, as the walks are appearing in the Chiltern Society's name, all the path numbers have been shown on the plans and incorporated into the texts. These numbers, which are also shown on the Society's Footpath Maps (where available), consist of the official County Council footpath number with the prefix letters used by the Society to indicate the parish concerned. It is therefore most helpful to use these when reporting any path problems you may find, together, if possible, with the national grid reference for the precise location of the trouble spot, as, in this way, the problem can be identified on the ground with a minimum of loss of time in looking for it. National grid references can, however, only be calculated with the help of Ordnance Survey Landranger or Pathfinder maps and an explanation of how this is done can be found in the Key to all Landranger maps.

The length of time required for any particular walk depends on a number of factors such as your personal walking speed, the number of hills, stiles, etc. to be negotiated, whether or not you stop to rest, eat or drink, investigate places of interest, etc. and the number of impediments such as mud, crops, overgrowth, ploughing, etc. which you encounter, but generally an average speed of between two and two and a half miles per hour is about right in the Chilterns. It is, however, always advisable to allow extra time if you are limited by the daylight or catching a particular bus or train home in order to avoid your walk developing into a race against the clock.

Should you have problems with any of the paths used on the walks or find that the description given is no longer correct, the author would be most grateful if you could let him have details (c/o The Book Castle), so that attempts can be made to rectify the problem or the text can be corrected at the next reprint. Nevertheless, the author hopes that you will not encounter any serious problems and have pleasure from following the walks.

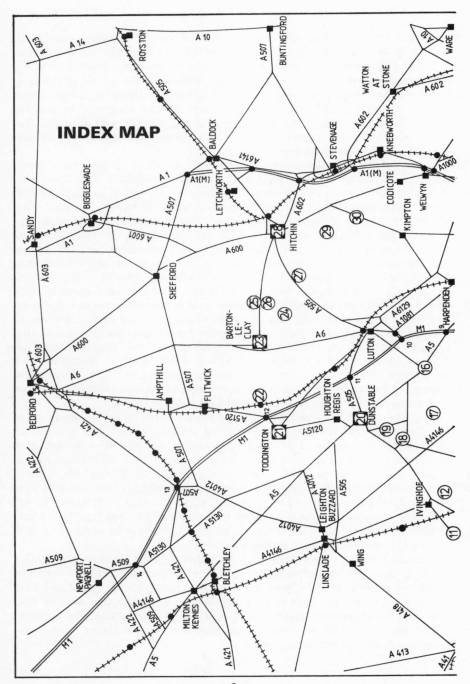

INDEX MAP

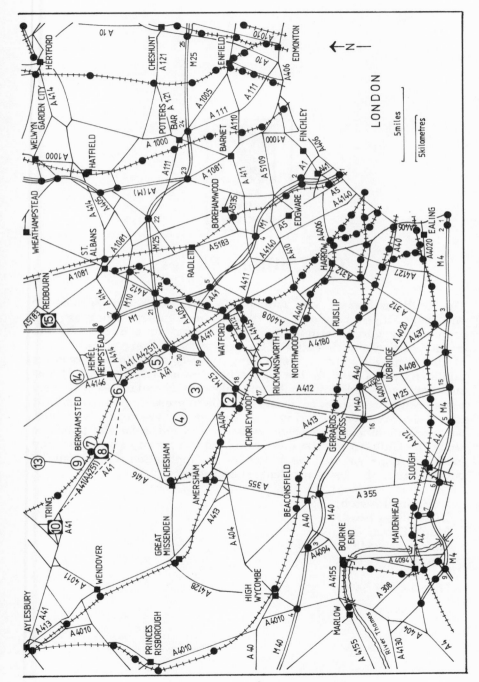

9

The Chiltern Society

The Chiltern Society

The Chiltern Society was founded in 1965 with the objects: 'To encourage high standards of town and country planning and architecture and to stimulate public interest in and care for the beauty, history and character of the area of the Chiltern Hills.'

The Society Rights of Way Group actively protects and restores public rights of way in the Chilterns – some 4,900 paths. It has surveyed every individual path and takes up irregularities with local parish councils, district or county councils to preserve public rights. It organises voluntary working parties most weekends to clear, waymark or otherwise encourage the use of paths for the public to enjoy the Chiltern countryside. Details of the Society's activities and footpath maps as well as membership application forms can be obtained from the Assistant General Secretary:

Christine Preston,
27 Chalfont Road,
Maple Cross,
Rickmansworth,
Herts WD3 2TA

(Tel: 0923–779988)

WALK 1: Rickmansworth (Batchworth)

Length of Walk: 7.1 miles / 11.4 Km

Starting Point: Roundabout at the junction of the A404 and A4145 at Batchworth on the edge of Rickmansworth.

Grid Ref: TQ064939

Maps: OS Landranger Sheet 176
OS Pathfinder Sheet TQ09/19

Parking: Cars can be parked in the service road alongside the A4145 (Moor Lane) at its junction with the A404. Access to this service road can be obtained from the roundabout.

Rickmansworth, familiarly known as 'Ricky', is situated at the confluence of three Chiltern rivers, the Colne, the Gade and the Chess. These waterways together with the presence of two ancient parks close to the town have ensured that its setting has remained relatively rural despite the rapid expansion which resulted from the coming of the Metropolitan Line in 1887. Indeed if one visits the old town centre with its narrow streets, which through-traffic now bypasses, it still retains its quiet country town atmosphere, even if the genuine old buildings have been supplemented by a number of modern imitations. The parish church, which was largely rebuilt in 1826 and 1890, retains its old tower dating from 1630 and a number of old brasses and monuments including the tomb of Sir Robert Carey, first Earl of Monmouth, who in 1603 rode to Holyrood to inform King James VI of Scotland of the death of Queen Elizabeth I and his consequent succession to the English throne. Other famous names associated with the town include Cardinal Wolsey, who owned Moor Park, William Penn, the prominent Quaker and founder of Pennsylvania, who lived at Basing House in the 1670s and the writer, George Eliot, who also lived in the town.

The walk, which is of a fairly easy nature, soon leaves the town behind and follows the Grand Union Canal towpath in its surprisingly rural setting to Springwell Lock before crossing the canal and continuing parallel to it to the edge of Harefield. It then climbs through a bluebell wood to Hill End and crosses

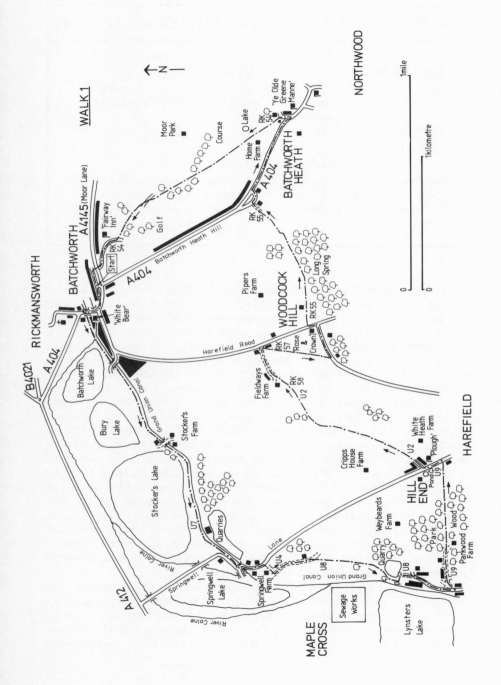

WALK 1

12

the hills to Woodcock Hill and Batchworth Heath with fine views at a number of points, before returning across Moor Park Golf Course with its splendid mansion to your point of departure.

Starting from the roundabout at the junction of the A404 and A4145 at Batchworth on the edge of Rickmansworth, follow the right-hand pavement of the A404 towards Rickmansworth for some 300 yards. After crossing the bridge over the Grand Union Canal, by Batchworth Lock House, turn right down a flight of steps to reach the canal towpath at Batchworth Lock. Here turn right passing under the A404 bridge and following the towpath straight on, soon leaving the town behind. After three-quarters of a mile, on reaching Stocker's Lock, to your left is Stocker's Farm which became famous as the set for the TV series of 'Black Beauty'. Just past the lock, go under a hump-backed bridge and continue to follow the towpath (later on path U7) for a further two-thirds of a mile, at one point passing a large boundary stone marking the boundary of Hertfordshire and the former county of Middlesex and then a derelict cement works.

On nearing Springwell Lock leave the towpath and join Springwell Lane to your right. Just past the lock follow the road turning left over Bridge No. 176, then turning right and climbing gently past a number of cottages with views of Springwell Lake, a flooded former gravel pit, to your right. Having passed the cottages, at a sharp left-hand bend where a right-hand crash-barrier ends, fork right onto fenced path U4. On reaching a track, turn left onto it and follow it gently uphill with wide views across the Colne valley towards the distant M25 opening out to your right. Just beyond some farm buildings, where the track bears left, leave it and take path U8 straight on over a stile by a gate. Now go straight on, keeping left of a fence and following this fence, later a hedge, to the far end of the field. Here cross a stile right of two gates and follow the top hedge of a field. At the far side of the field, turn right and follow a left-hand fence downhill through a tree belt with an old gravel pit now used as a firing range to your left to reach a stile. Cross this and follow an obvious winding path through scrubland between the quarry and the canal bank eventually reaching the quarry entrance. Here turn right onto a track, soon passing a padlocked gate to enter a factory car park on the edge of Harefield.

Go straight on through the car park to join a road called Summerhouse Lane, then follow it straight on between factories, soon rejoining the canal bank. Where further factories commence to your right, turn left onto a concrete road (path U9) and follow it, ignoring branching tracks to your left. On reaching some terraced cottages, disregard a right-hand fork and take the access road straight on uphill passing the cottages and a smallholding. At the gates of Parkwood Farm Kennels, leave the road and go straight on between anti-horse barriers into a fenced path which climbs through Park Wood, in early May a mass of bluebells. At the top of the hill, cross a footbridge over a spring, then take the fenced path straight on between fields to a road at Hill End.

Cross this road and turn left along its pavement passing the 'Plough', then opposite a large pond turn right onto path U2, an access road to a number of houses. At the far end of this road go straight on over a stile into a field, then bear slightly left following a worn path beside a depression in the ground across the field to cross a stile. Here bear slightly left and follow a left-hand hedge. Where the hedge bears left, leave it and go straight on to cross a stile under a tree in a corner of the field. Now follow a left-hand hedge straight on downhill to stile and footbridge, then follow a crop break straight on uphill to cross a stile at the county boundary. Here take path RK58 beside a left-hand hedge to Fieldways Farm where you join the farm drive and follow it straight on. Just before reaching Harefield Road, turn sharp right through a fence gap onto path RK57 crossing a field diagonally to pass just left of a telegraph pole and cross a stile just left of the far corner of the field. Now bear half right across the corner of the next field to cross a stile by a white gate, then cross a further field diagonally to a stile in the far corner leading to Harefield Road opposite a county boundary stone.

Turn left onto this road, then at a road junction by the 'Rose and Crown' at Woodcock Hill turn left. Opposite the pub car park turn right onto fenced path RK55. Where this emerges over low rails into a field with fine views ahead towards Batchworth Heath, go straight on downhill to a hedge gap in the bottom corner, then follow the outside edge of a wood called Long Spring downhill. At the bottom of the hill, leave the right-hand hedge and go straight on across the field to cross a stile in the far corner. Now turn right and follow a right-hand hedge through two fields. Where the hedge ends, cross a stile by a five-bar gate and follow a fenced path uphill to reach a layby on the A404 at Batchworth Heath Hill. Turn right into the layby and where it ends, cross the A404, turn right onto its pavement and follow it uphill to Batchworth Heath.

At the top of the hill turn left into Park Close. Where the road turns right, leave it and take enclosed path RK54 straight on between private drives, soon emerging onto Moor Park Golf Course. Here go straight on, following a series of four-foot wooden marker posts with white arrows passing left of a small lake and crossing several fairways. Having traversed a small copse, there is a fine view to your right of Moor Park mansion. Described by Sir Niklaus Pevsner as 'the grandest eighteenth-century mansion in Hertfordshire', Moor Park is, in fact, a seventeenth-century house which was remodelled in the Palladian style for the merchant Benjamin Styles by the architect Sir James Thornhill between 1725 and 1727 with a rich rococo interior and a large classical portico. The house, which had, before its remodelling, been the home of the ill-fated Duke of Monmouth, was acquired by Rickmansworth UDC in 1937 and is now almost certainly the most magnificent golf clubhouse in the country.

Continue to follow the marker posts straight on, passing a bench, then right of a copse, then left of a second copse to join a macadam drive by a gnarled oak tree. Follow this drive for about 50 yards then fork right, following the marker posts diagonally across a fairway, then bearing slightly left to pass through a gap in a tree belt and continue downhill to rejoin the macadam drive. Turn right onto this and follow it past the 'Fairway Inn' and on to the A4145. Cross this road carefully, then turn left for your starting point.

WALK 2: Chorleywood

Length of Walk: (A) 6.9 miles / 11.1 Km
                       (B) 5.8 miles / 9.3 Km

Starting Point: Car park on south side of A404 by Chorleywood Cricket Pavilion.

Grid Ref: TQ034967

Maps: OS Landranger Sheets 166 or 176
            OS Pathfinder Sheet TQ09/19
            Chiltern Society FP Map No. 5

How to get there / Parking: Chorleywood, 2 miles northwest of Rickmansworth, may be reached by leaving the M25 at Junction 18 and taking the A404 towards Amersham. Having passed Chorleywood Church on your left, the car park by the cricket pavilion is some 300 yards beyond on your left.

Notes: Heavy nettle growth may be encountered at several points on both walks in the summer months, while bridleway CN3 is prone to deep mud in places, even in dry weather.

Chorleywood, with its 200-acres partially wooded common, is perhaps a typical example of the curious mixture of countryside and suburbia found in what was once called 'Metroland'. To the east and west of the common are sizeable built-up areas which have grown up since the Metropolitan Railway reached the village in 1889, while the spacious common itself is surrounded by typical Chiltern cottages and on the edge of the village is the farmhouse where the Quaker, William Penn, who later founded the American state of Pennsylvania, was married in 1672.

Both walks first lead you across the common to the built-up area around Chorleywood Station before leaving the village and passing through pleasant beechwoods and a long green lane to the outskirts of Chenies. Here Walk B leads you through the village before dropping into the Chess valley at Sarratt Bottom, while Walk A makes a gradual and scenic descent into the Chess valley at the picture-book village of Latimer. It then turns to follow the Chess valley downstream past the ruins of the old Flaunden Church as well as Dodds Mill to rejoin Walk B. Both walks then climb to Sarratt Church before returning across the Chess valley and through Chorleywood Park to your starting point.

Both walks start from the car park by Chorleywood Cricket Pavilion on the south side of the A404 and take path CW32b, a wide glade leading from the rear of the car park across the wooded common. On emerging from the trees, go straight on until you reach a worn crossing path. Turn left onto this path, which is later marked as a 'horse track' and follow it, ignoring a fork to the left at one point, until you reach Common Road at a gap in the houses by a bus stop left of the 'Rose and Crown'. Cross the road here and take path CW15, a macadam lane called Colley Land, straight on downhill. This later narrows to a path and reaches another road by the Metropolitan Line embankment. Turn right onto this road then immediately left under a railway bridge. At a crossroads by a shopping parade, turn right and at a fork, go right again into the continuation of Whitelands Avenue. Ignore two branching roads to the left, then between 59 and 61 Whitelands Avenue, turn left onto fenced path CW–CN2 ducking under a rail and taking the path into Carpenter's Wood.

On reaching the wood, turn immediately right and follow back garden fences along the edge of the wood. Where the gardens end, go straight on through Whitelands Wood, soon walking parallel to and later joining a permissive bridleway. At the far side of the wood turn right onto bridleway CN3 passing either side of a gate then under a railway bridge. Now take a hedged green lane straight on for over half a mile, passing through Halsey's Wood and eventually reaching the A404 at Chenies Turn. Here cross the A404 and turn left onto its pavement, following it for some 200 yards, then turn right onto path CN34, the rough drive to Great House Farm, with wide views of the Chess valley to your left and of Chenies Manor House, rebuilt by the first Earl of Bedford in 1530, and the outskirts of the village to your right.

On reaching a fork, **Walk B** turns right onto bridleway CN35 and follows this, then the village street, straight on to the picturesque village green. Here, at a fork, leave the road and bear half right across the green heading for a macadam lane left of a white cottage with lattice windows where you join **Walk 4A**. Now see the text of **Walk 4**.

At the junction of CN34/CN35, **Walk 2A** takes bridleway CN35 straight on to the start of a left-hand copse. Here turn left onto path CN48, passing through the gates of 'The Farm House', then turning immediately right over a stile. Now follow an obvious path through the copse to a stile. Cross this, a farm road and another stile opposite and take path CN42 straight on through a wood. At a fork bear left to cross a stile at the edge of the wood with a fine view of Latimer nestling in the Chess valley ahead. Here turn right over a second stile, then turn left and gradually diverge from the left-hand fence to cross a further stile. Now go straight on across the next field to reach the top corner of Coney Wood. Here follow the top edge of this wood, later a right-hand hedge to enter a corner of Walk Wood. Just inside the wood, turn right over a stile where you obtain a fine view of Latimer and the Chess valley with Latimer House partially hidden in trees on the wooded hill to your left.

Latimer, until the nineteenth century variously known as 'Isenhampstead Cheynduit' or 'Isenhampstead Latimer', was formerly a hamlet of Chesham belonging to the Cavendish family (later the Lords Chesham) of Latimer House. The original house, where Charles I was held prisoner in 1647, was largely rebuilt in the nineteenth century in neo-Tudor style. The village church was also rebuilt in 1841 and renovated by Sir George Gilbert Scott in 1867, while many of the picturesque village cottages also date from this period.

Now bear half left across the field to a stile in the bottom left-hand corner leading to a crossroads. Cross the stile and the B485 and take the road signposted to Latimer and Flaunden straight on to a bridge over the River Chess by a weir. At the far end of the bridge, turn right through a green gate onto path LT20 and follow a right-hand fence parallel to the river. At one point you pass through a marshy area where it is generally drier closer to the riverbank, then follow a right-hand fence (soon on bridleway CN56) eventually passing a clump of trees to your right which conceals the ruins of the old Flaunden church. This thirteenth-century church was abandoned in 1838 when a new church was built in the hilltop village of Flaunden more than a mile away. Although the old church was still used for occasional services, it was already a ruin by the late nineteenth century and very little of it now remains. On reaching a gate and stile at the far left-hand corner of the field, cross the stile and follow a left-hand fence to an old tomb shaded by two oaks. Here go straight on for a third of a mile, soon passing through a gate and continuing to Mill Farm at Chenies Bottom (where home-made ice-cream is on sale), then go straight on through the farmyard to a road near Dodds Mill.

Walks 2A and 4B turn left onto the road and follow it to a left-hand bend. Here leave the road and take path CN60 straight on over a stile by a gate then along the top of a slight bank marking the edge of the flood plain. Having crossed a stile, go straight on, crossing another stile at the far side of the field and following a left-hand hedge to a stile into Limeshill Wood. Now take path SA37 straight on

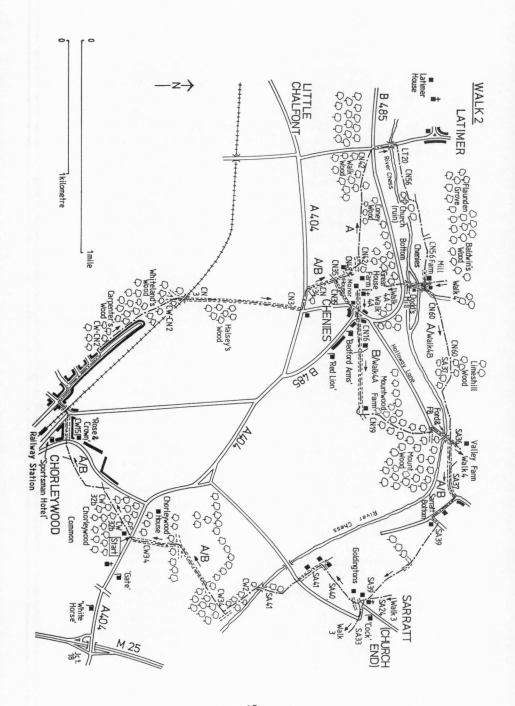

WALK 2

LATIMER

LITTLE CHALFONT

CHENIES

CHORLEYWOOD

SARRATT (CHURCH END)

19

through the wood to cross a stile into a field where you bear half right and follow a right-hand fence to the banks of the River Chess. Here turn left and follow the edge of the riverside marsh to a gate and stile, then bear slightly right across a field to a stile leading to a junction of concrete roads by a ford and footbridge over the Chess, where **Walk 4B** turns left onto path SA36 rejoining **Walk 4A** (now return to the text of **Walk 4**), while **Walk 2A** takes path SA37 straight on rejoining **Walk 2B**.

Walks 2A and 2B now follow the concrete road straight on for a quarter mile to a bend in a road by some cottages at Sarratt Bottom. Turn right onto this road and at a junction turn left past a white cottage. Some 50 yards beyond the cottage, turn right through a kissing-gate onto path SA39 and follow a right-hand hedge to a stile. Cross this and bear slightly left across a field to the far left-hand corner. Here ignore a stile to your left and bear slightly right into a tree-lined lane, following this uphill. Near the top, go straight on over a stile by a gate into a field and follow its right-hand hedge. At the far side of the field bear half right through a kissing-gate into Sarratt churchyard (briefly joining **Walk 3**) and take a gravel path passing right of the twelfth-century church (described in the introduction to **Walk 3**).

At a fork in the path, go right (leaving **Walk 3** again), passing through a handgate and taking path SA40 straight on over a stile. Now follow a left-hand fence then a right-hand hedge to the macadam drive to an early nineteenth-century manor house called Goldingtons. Cross the drive and a stile, with a fine view of the Chess valley ahead, and follow a right-hand fence straight on downhill to cross a stile near a cottage and join its drive. Now follow this, turning left onto path SA41 to reach a road. Cross this and go through a fence gap opposite, then follow a right-hand hedge straight on to the far end of the field. Here go straight on through a fence gap then turn right into a thicket and follow a left-hand fence beside a poplar copse to a footbridge over a very picturesque section of the River Chess. Just beyond the end of this footbridge, turn left over a stile onto path CW2 into a belt of trees. Disregarding a fork to the left, take an obvious path straight on for about 350 yards to a T-junction of paths at the far end of the tree-belt. Here turn right over a stile onto path CW34 into a wood and follow a well-defined path uphill, eventually joining a track which soon enters an avenue of trees in Chorleywood Park. Follow this avenue to its far end, then at a junction of tracks, turn right. On reaching a macadam drive, turn left onto it and follow it, with Chorleywood House soon coming into view to your right, until you reach gates leading to the A404 directly opposite your starting point.

WALK 3: Sarratt

Length of Walk: 6.3 miles / 10.1 Km
Starting Point: 'The Boot', Sarratt Green.
Grid Ref: TQ042996
Maps: OS Landranger Sheets 166 or 176
OS Pathfinder Sheet TQ09/19
(part only) Chiltern Society FP Map No. 5

How to get there / Parking: Sarratt Green, 3.5 miles north of Rickmansworth, may be reached by leaving the M25 at Junction 18 and taking the A404 towards Amersham. After 1 mile turn right onto a road signposted to Sarratt and follow it for 1.6 miles to a crossroads near the 'Cricketers' at Sarratt Green. Here turn left and find a suitable parking space along the quiet service road on the left side of the village green.

Notes: Heavy nettle growth may be encountered at several points in the summer months and part of path SA24 is prone to deep mud even in dry weather.

Sarratt, despite its close proximity to the M25 and the large built-up areas of Watford and Rickmansworth, has a remarkably rural setting. The traditional Chiltern cottages of what is now the main village at Sarratt Green are ranged around an attractive and unusually long green with a duckpond at one end, while the ancient village known as Church End about two-thirds of a mile away on the northern slopes of the Chess valley now has little more than the church, a pub, a nineteenth-century manor house and some almshouses rebuilt in the same period. The cruciform twelfth-century church, appropriately dedicated to the Holy Cross, is particularly interesting as its tower was rebuilt in the fifteenth century in part with Roman bricks (presumably emanating from the ruins of a Roman villa discovered in the vicinity) and it is also the only church tower in Hertfordshire to have a saddleback roof. The church, restored by Sir George Gilbert Scott in 1865, also contains a Norman font, a fragment of a thirteenth-century wall-painting and a carved Jacobean pulpit, from which the renowned Nonconformist Richard Baxter preached in the seventeenth century.

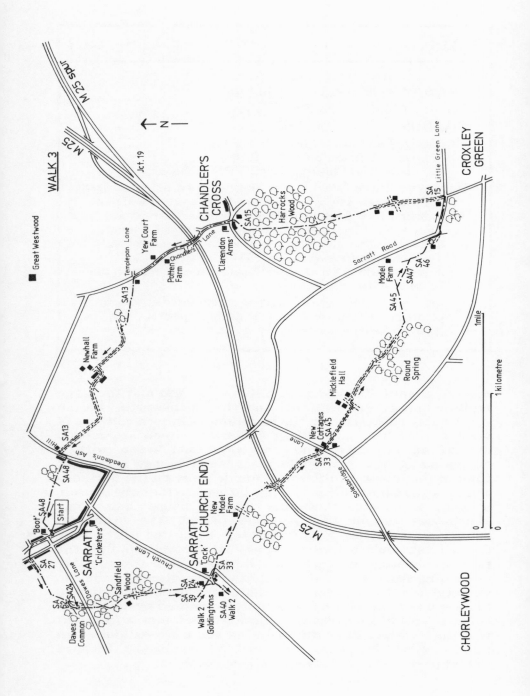

WALK 3

M25 spur

M25

Jct. 19

← N —

■ Great Westwood

CHANDLER'S CROSS

Yew Court Farm

Templepan Lane

Chandlers Lane

Potten Farm

'Clarendon Arms'

SA15

SA15

Harrocks Wood

Little Green Lane

CROXLEY GREEN

SA 15

Sarratt Road

SA46

SA47

Model Farm

SA45

Newhall Farm

SA13

SA13

Deadman's Ash Hill

SA48

SA48

'Boot'

Start

SARRATT

'Cricketers'

Mickefield Hall

Round Spring

New Cottages

SA 45

SA 33

Solesbridge Lane

M25

SARRATT (CHURCH END)

'Cock'

SA 33

New Model Farm

Church Lane

SA/62 SA24

Dawes Common

Dawes Lane

SA 27

Sandfield Wood

SA SA 39 24

Walk 2 Goldingtons

SA40 Walk 2

1mile

1 kilometre

0

0

CHORLEYWOOD

22

The walk, which explores the surprisingly remote hilltop plateau between Watford and the Chess valley with its bluebell woods, leads you from Sarratt Green via the wooded Dawes Common to Church End, near which fine views open out from time to time across the Chess valley. It then takes you over the M25 and via Micklefield Hall to the edge of Croxley Green, before returning by way of Chandler's Cross to Sarratt Green.

Starting from the 'Boot' pub on the northeast side of Sarratt Green, take the road along the edge of the green northwestwards to its junction with the road to Commonwood, then bear half left across the green, passing left of a pond to reach a path signposted to Dawes Lane (SA27). Take this path along a gravel lane, ignoring branching drives to your right, to cross a stile by a gate at the far end. Now bear slightly right across a field to the corner of a hedge ahead, then follow the left-hand hedge until it turns left. Here bear half left across the field to cross a stile by a gate in the field corner into the wooded Dawes Common. In the wood, take a gravel track (path SA52) straight on, soon swinging left by a right-hand gate and stile onto path SA24 to reach Dawes Lane.

Cross this road and a stile by a gate opposite and take path SA24 straight on through woodland, soon passing between fenced plantations then entering mature woodland. Now at a fork take the right-hand option which soon passes through a kissing-gate and follows a right-hand hedge along the edge of Sandfield Wood to a further kissing-gate by a house leading onto a gravel track. Take this track straight on along the edge of the wood, ignoring a crossing track, then at a left-hand bend, take path SA24 straight on through another kissing-gate and follow the edge of a left-hand wood with fine views of the Chess valley to your right. At a corner of the wood go straight on across a field, with Sarratt Church soon coming into view ahead, to reach a kissing-gate into the churchyard. Go through this kissing-gate (briefly joining **Walk 2**) and follow a gravel path passing right of the church.

At a fork in the path keep left, leaving **Walk 2** and going through a lychgate into Church Lane. Turn right onto this road and follow it round a left-hand bend. At a sharp right-hand bend leave the road and take path SA33 straight on through a gate. Now follow the edge of a wood downhill with a view to your right across the Chess valley to Chorleywood. At the bottom corner of the field, turn right then after a few yards turn left through some iron railings and over a stile. Here bear half right across a field, climbing to a hedge gap just right of the right-hand of two oaks ahead. Now go straight on across the next field to a fence and hedge gap right of New Model Farm. Go straight on across the next field to join a left-hand hedge at a slight bend in it then follow this hedge downhill to a stile onto a track near a bridge over the M25. Turn right onto this track, then immediately left over the bridge. At the far end of the bridge, cross a stile in the right-hand fence, then resume your previous direction, taking a track straight on beside a left-hand hedge for a quarter mile, eventually passing through two gates to reach Solesbridge Lane by New Cottages.

Cross this road and take path SA45, a rough fenced track, straight on for some 300 yards to a concreted farmyard at Micklefield Hall. Go straight on through the farmyard and a gate, then turn left onto a concrete farm road to pass through another gate. Now turn right into a hedged lane (still SA45) and follow it straight on for a third of a mile, soon entering a wood called Round Spring where you ignore the two right-hand branching tracks into the wood. On leaving the wood and emerging into a field, follow a right-hand tree-belt straight on to its end. Here bear half left across the field to a stile. Cross this and bear slightly right onto path SA47 following a right-hand hedge to cross another stile at the far end of the field. Now take path SA46 straight on across the next field to a further stile, then bear half left across another field to a stile left of a flagpole leading into a garden. Here go straight on keeping left of an ornamental hedge to reach a roadside hedge, then follow this hedge, later joining a macadam drive to reach a bend in Sarratt Road. Now take this road straight on to its junction with Little Green Lane on the edge of Croxley Green.

Here turn left onto path SA15, a rough farm road and follow it beside a left-hand hedge for a quarter mile. At a crossways go straight on, then ignore a signposted path to the right and bear slightly left into a hedged lane. On reaching a timber-framed single-storey cottage, take a narrow hedged path straight on. This becomes a fenced path along the edge of a field and ultimately reaches a squeeze-stile into Harrocks Wood. Follow an obvious path straight on through this wood and at the far side of the wood take a fenced path straight on to a road junction by the 'Clarendon Arms' at Chandler's Cross.

Here cross the major road and take Chandler's Lane straight on uphill for half a mile, recrossing the M25 and passing Potten Farm and Yew Court Farm with its attractive timber buildings and courtyard. At the junction with Templepan Lane, turn left over a stile onto path SA13 and cross a field diagonally heading for the left-hand end of a copse. On reaching the copse, follow its edge to a macadam farm road, then turn left onto it and follow it to Newhall Farm. Here turn left by a black barn, keeping the barn to your right, then at the far end of the barn, turn right onto a concrete farm road between the barn and a left-hand tractor shed. Follow this concrete road (still

SA13) straight on, leaving the farm and after nearly half a mile reaching a road at Sarratt called Deadman's Ash Hill. Turn left onto this road and follow it for about 100 yards, then at the end of a right-hand hedge, turn right onto the macadam drive to numbers 1 to 4 The Old Cottages. Where this drive forks, cross a stile in the middle of the fork and take fenced path SA48 straight on to cross a stile at the far end of the right-hand garden. Here go straight on across a field to cross a stile in the far left-hand corner, then cross the next field diagonally to a stile by the far hedge into a fenced path which leads you out to Sarratt Green near the 'Boot'.

WALK 4: Flaunden

Length of Walk: (A) 6.6 miles / 10.7 Km
(B) 6.1 miles / 9.8 Km

Starting Point: Flaunden village hall car park.

Grid Ref: TL017008

Maps: OS Landranger Sheet 166
OS Pathfinder Sheets TL00/10 & TQ09/19
Chiltern Society FP Map No. 5

How to get there / Parking: Flaunden, 5 miles northwest of Rickmansworth, may be reached by leaving the M25 at Junction 18 and taking the A404 through Chorleywood towards Amersham. After 1.6 miles turn right onto a road signposted to Chenies and Latimer and follow its winding course for 1.5 miles passing through Chenies and descending into the Chess valley. At a crossroads turn right onto the Latimer and Flaunden road and follow it straight on for 2 miles to reach Flaunden. Here ignore a branching road to the right, then at the village crossroads, turn right and the car park by the village hall is about 100 yards ahead on your left.

Notes: Both alternative walks are prone to heavy nettle growth in summer and deep in mud in places even in dry weather.

Flaunden, locally pronounced 'Flarnden', is an unspoilt secluded village clustered around a crossroads of narrow lanes on a hilltop north of the Chess valley. The village church, built in 1838 to replace a thirteenth-century predecessor over a mile away in the Chess valley, is notable for being the first to be designed by the celebrated architect, Sir George Gilbert Scott, who was later responsible for the Midland Grand Hotel in London which forms the façade of St. Pancras Station. This church incorporates several items from its predecessor including its fifteenth-century font, three ancient bells and the one-handed church clock.

Both walks, which are characterised by a mixture of fine views and pleasant woodland, lead you down into the idyllically rural Chess valley at Chenies Bottom, where Walk B follows the valley bottom, while Walk A crosses into Bucks.

and climbs a wooded hillside to visit the picturesque feudal village of Chenies. After Walk A drops again to rejoin Walk B, both routes return to Flaunden by way of the quiet hamlet of Belsize nestling in a Chiltern hollow.

Both walks start from the entrance to Flaunden village hall car park, turning right onto the road and following it to the village crossroads. Here turn left onto the road signposted to Latimer and Chesham. Go past the 'Green Dragon' then at a road junction by the church, fork left into a cul-de-sac road (joining the reverse direction of Bucks. Walk 8) and follow it for nearly half a mile to a fork by wooden gates. Here fork left onto hedged bridleway FD8 (leaving Bucks. Walk 8 again). After some 25 yards turn right over a stile and take path FD2 beside a left-hand hedge to cross a stile at Martin Top Farm.

Now turn left onto bridleway FD6 between the farm buildings, crossing a concrete road and taking a fenced bridleway straight on across a field. At the far side of the field follow the bridleway turning right to reach a concrete farm road. Now take path FD2a straight on over a stile following a right-hand fence, later the outside edge of Baldwin's Wood, gradually descending with views of the Chess valley ahead and Sarratt Church and Goldingtons on a hilltop to your left, to reach a crossing track. Cross this and a stile with wide views of the Chess valley opening out ahead, then take path CN59 straight on downhill, passing just left of an oak tree to reach two stiles leading into a farmyard at Mill Farm. Now go straight on through the farmyard to a gate onto the road in Chenies Bottom, where you meet Walk 2A. (NB. Home-made ice-cream is sold at the farm!)

Walk B turns left here onto the road joining Walk 2A. Now see the text of Walk 2. Walk A bears slightly right onto the road crossing two bridges over arms of the Chess and passing Dodd's Mill, then where the road forks, keep right. At a T-junction, cross the B485 and take path CN37 into the wood opposite. Just inside the wood, fork left and take a winding path uphill ignoring branching paths to your right to cross a stile. Now take a hedged, later walled path uphill past Chenies Church to the gates of Chenies Manor House. The church to your left dates from the fifteenth century and is principally notable for the Russell family chapel which was added a century later and houses numerous monuments to the Earls and Dukes of Bedford and other members of the Russell family. The Manor to your right was rebuilt by the first Earl of Bedford in 1530 and was, at one time, known as Chenies Palace, possibly due to both Henry VIII and Elizabeth I staying there several times. The village, whose name derives from the Cheynes family, from whom it passed to the Russells by female succession in 1526, was originally known as Isenhampstead and then

Isenhampstead Cheynes. Its name only contracted to its present form in the nineteenth century when a benevolent Duke of Bedford also had many of its cottages rebuilt or improved.

By the Manor gates turn left down the drive to the picturesque village green. At a crossways, bear slightly left across the green heading for a macadam lane left of a white cottage. Here **Walks 2B and 4A** cross the B485 and follow the lane (path CN16) straight on out of the village for nearly half a mile, at one point passing through gates. On reaching Mountwood Farm, by some white wooden rails fork right onto a fenced grassy path swinging left. Where this path joins a stony track, turn immediately left over a stile onto path CN19 and bear slightly right across a field to a stile into Mount Wood. In the wood take a waymarked path straight on downhill joining a right-hand fence by the corner of a field and following it downhill to reach a crossing track. Turn left onto this and follow it to Holloway Lane then turn right onto this road to reach a ford and footbridge over the Chess. Cross the bridge and a stile, then **Walk 2B** turns right onto a farm road (path SA37) rejoining Walk 2A (now see text of Walk 2); while **Walk 4A** rejoins **Walk 4B** taking path SA36 straight on along the farm road.

At Valley Farm **Walks 4A and 4B** fork right by an oak tree following a right-hand fence to a gate into a hedged path. Take this path straight on, crossing a stile at one point, then ignore a crossing path and bear slightly left into the continuation of the hedged path leading to a stile into Hanginglane Wood. Here take the obvious path straight on, at one point joining a track and following it to the far side of the wood. Now ignore a crossing track and take a stony track straight on through a tree belt. At the far end of the tree belt you currently have to take a *de facto* route continuing along the track to a T-junction with a concrete road near Rosehall Farm where you rejoin the official right of way.

Turn right onto this road (path SA25) and where its concrete surface ends, fork right onto a farm road soon passing Rosehall Wood. At the far side of the wood, where the farm road turns left, leave it, forking right over a stile between a gate and an oak tree and heading for a house visible through a hedge gap right of a pylon to cross a stile in the next hedge. Now bear half left to a gate by the corner of a hedge then bear half left again to a stile just right of some power-lines. Cross this and turn left onto a road. Just past a cottage, turn right through a hedge gap into Plough Wood, then fork immediately left onto waymarked path SA21 and follow it diagonally across the wood, ignoring a crossing track, then crossing a stile into a field corner. Here follow the outside edge of the wood straight on, then at a corner of the wood, bear half right across the field to a stile onto Poles Hill at Belsize.

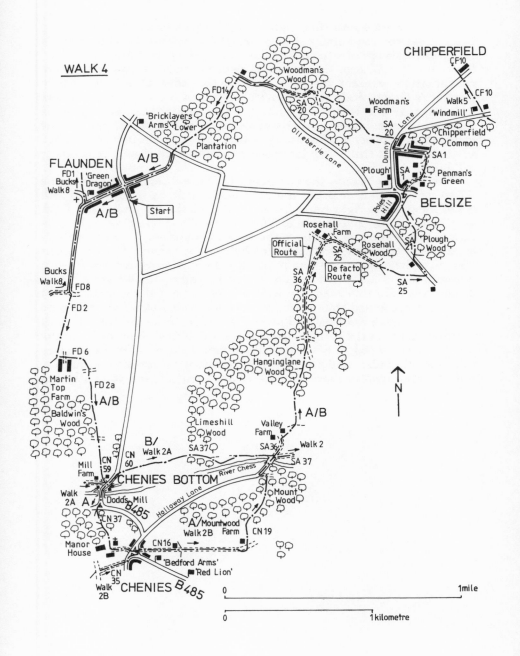

WALK 4

FLAUNDEN

CHIPPERFIELD

BELSIZE

CHENIES BOTTOM

CHENIES

29

Cross this road and turn right along its pavement. At a left-hand bend, cross the road again and go straight on across the village green to an entrance left of a telephone box. Here take path SA1, a concreted lane, uphill. Where its concrete surface ends, follow its rough continuation straight on to a fork at the edge of a wood called Penman's Green. Here fork left onto a track into the wood and where it forks, take the lesser right-hand option straight on, soon passing through an anti-horse barrier and joining a gravel drive. Follow this straight on between gateposts, then turn left onto a rough road called Little Windmill Hill which later becomes macadamed and descends to a T-junction.

Here turn right onto the pavement of Dunny Lane and after some 60 yards, turn left crossing the road and a stile by a gate onto path SA20 following a right-hand hedge uphill. At the far end of the field, go straight on into a corner of Woodman's Wood, keeping right at a fork to follow the inside edge of the wood straight on. Where woodland commences to your right, take the obvious path straight on for about 200 yards ignoring a crossing path. At a T-junction with a track, turn left onto it and follow it to a gate and stile leading to Olleberrie Lane. Turn right onto this road and follow it for some 350 yards, then just past a cottage called Hollow Hedge, turn left over a stile by a gate onto path FD14 into a wood called Lower Plantation. Take the obvious path straight on along the inside edge of the wood at first, then through the middle of the wood to reach a stile leading to a road junction. Here take the Flaunden and Chenies road straight on for over a quarter mile to Flaunden crossroads, where you turn left for your starting point.

WALK 5: King's Langley

Length of Walk: 6.8 miles / 11.0 Km

Starting Point: Crossroads near King's Langley cricket pitch.

Grid Ref: TL066028

Maps: OS Landranger Sheet 166
OS Pathfinder Sheet TL00/10
(part only) Chiltern Society FP Map No. 5

How to get there / Parking: King's Langley, 2.5 miles southeast of Hemel Hempstead, may be reached from the town by taking the old A41 (A4251) towards Watford. In the village centre, turn right into Vicarage Lane (signposted to Chipperfield, Sarratt and Bovingdon) and follow it uphill for 750 yards. Just past the cricket pitch to your right, turn right at a crossroads into Love Lane, where there is a parking area on the edge of the common immediately on your right.

Notes: At the time of writing, work had not started on the A41 King's Langley Bypass which is due for completion shortly after publication in 1993. The walk description in its vicinity is therefore only based on plans for the new road and so may be somewhat inaccurate. When the new road opens, the old A41 is to be renumbered A4251. Heavy nettle growth may be encountered in summer particularly on path KL5.

King's Langley, on the western slopes of the Gade valley, now has its centre along the old A41 (A4251) near which can be found the fifteenth-century parish church. This was, however, not always the case, as the thirteenth-century royal palace and early fourteenth-century priory were both situated at the top of the hill. Indeed, in mediaeval times the village was for more than two centuries at the centre of the national stage. King's Langley Palace was built for Queen Eleanor, wife of Edward I, whose son, later to become Edward II, was brought up here and as king frequently stayed here. In 1315, Edward II had his lifelong friend Piers Gaveston buried at the Priory some two years after the latter had been beheaded by the Earl of Warwick. Another prominent victim of a violent death to be buried at the Priory was Richard II, but his remains were later

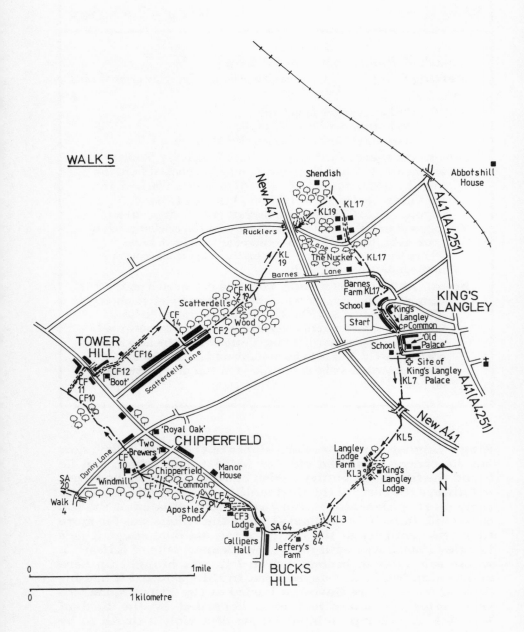

WALK 5

Abbotshill House

Shendish

New A41

A41 (A4251)

KL17
KL19

Rucklers

Lane

KL19

The Nucker
Lane
Barnes
Lane

KL17

KL17

Barnes
Farm KL17

School

KING'S
LANGLEY

Start

King's
Langley
cp Common

CF KL
19

Scatterdells

Wood

CF
14

CF2

School

'Old
Palace'

Site of
King's Langley
Palace

KL7

A41 (A4251)

TOWER
HILL

CF16

Scatterdells Lane

CF12

CF
11

'Boot'

CF10

New A41

KL5

'Royal Oak'

CHIPPERFIELD

Two
Brewers'

CF
10

'Windmill'

Dunny Lane

Chipperfield

CF
4

Common

CF

Manor
House

Langley
Lodge
Farm

King's
Langley
Lodge

KL3

SA
20

Walk
4

Apostles
Pond

CF4

CF3
Lodge

SA 64

KL3

N

Callipers
Hall

Jeffery's
Farm

SA
64

BUCKS
HILL

0   1 mile

0   1 kilometre

32

removed by Henry V for reburial in Westminster Abbey. Prince Edmund de Langley, the fifth son of Edward III, who was later made the first Duke of York, was born at the Palace in 1341 and buried at the Priory in 1402, but when the latter was suppressed during the Reformation, his remains were moved to the parish church, where his tomb can still be seen today. Part of the Palace was destroyed by fire in the fifteenth century, after which it declined in importance. Today, little remains of this mediaeval royal residence and of the Priory, only one building has survived which is now part of Rudolf Steiner School.

The walk takes you from the attractive common of King's Langley past the sites of the Priory and the Palace across the open, rolling hills southwest of the village to Chipperfield with its wooded common before returning by way of Tower Hill and Shendish to King's Langley.

Starting from the crossroads of Vicarage Lane, Love Lane, Langley Hill and Chipperfield Road, take Langley Hill downhill past the site of the Priory. At a sharp left-hand bend by a pub called the 'Old Palace', turn right; then, by the entrance to Rudolf Steiner School, turn left onto path KL7, a narrow alleyway right of a garage, passing between hedges to a stile. Cross this, with a fine view ahead across the Gade valley spanned by the M25 viaduct to Abbot's Langley and the Colne valley beyond, then go straight on across a field to cross a stile at the top of the next rise. Now turn right onto path KL8 and follow a right-hand fence to a stile in the corner of the field. Do not cross this, but turn left and follow a right-hand fence to a footbridge over the new A41. At its far end, turn left onto path KL5, following the A41 fence for some 30 yards. Now bear right and follow a right-hand fence to a stile. Cross this and bear half right across a field heading for Langley Lodge Farm to cross a stile, then follow a left-hand fence to a stile into a plantation. Go straight on through the plantation to a stile leading to a junction of concrete roads by the farm.

Take the middle option (path KL3) straight on past a Georgian house, then bearing left between large ponds with an imposing house called Kings Langley Lodge hidden in the trees to your left. By a modern house and farm buildings, turn right, keeping the farm buildings to your left and the house to your right, to leave the farm by way of a stile by a gate. Now take a fenced farm track straight on downhill, ignoring stiles in both fences. At the end of this track, follow a left-hand fence and sporadic hedge virtually straight on downhill to cross a stile in a thick hedge. Now bear half-left uphill across a field to a hedge gap at the left-hand end of a clump of trees. Go through this gap and turn right onto a sunken track (bridleway SA64). Follow this uphill for about 300 yards, then, after it levels off, at a left-hand bend just short of Jeffrey's Farm, the reputed home of President Jimmy Carter's ancestors, leave the track and take path SA64, heading half-right across a field towards a tall redwood tree on the skyline, to reach the corner of a garden hedge. Here bear half right again to a stile and hedge gap onto a road called Bucks Hill near Chipperfield Common virtually opposite Callipers Lodge.

Turn right onto this road and follow it to a sharp left-hand bend by the Chipperfield village nameboard. Here turn left onto path CF3, the left-hand of two tracks, following the back of Chipperfield's wooded common until you reach two cottages. Go past the first of these cottages, then, by an old gateway leading to three garages, turn right onto a narrow path into the woods (CF4). At a T-junction of paths, turn left, soon passing a pond to your left and going straight on to reach the Apostles' Pond. This pond is so named because it used to be surrounded by twelve ancient lime trees which had to be replaced by young trees in 1984 which will take some years to mature. Go straight on past this pond, then, at a fork, take the left-hand option. Follow this path straight on through the woods for nearly half a mile, ignoring all crossing paths, until houses come into sight ahead. Here at a fork, take the left-hand option to reach a road at Chipperfield by a signpost just right of the 'Windmill' pub which stands on or near the site of a windmill shown on the 1822 Ordnance Survey map. The village church built in 1837 and the other village pubs can be reached by taking the road to your right.

Cross this road and take the narrow, fenced path CF10 between gardens to a stile into a field. Now go straight on downhill to a gate and stile in front of the last house in a row in Dunny Lane. Bear slightly left across this road to cross another stile by a gate, then follow a right-hand hedge uphill through a field to a derelict kissing gate. Go through this and continue to follow the right-hand hedge, turning left then right. On entering a copse, go straight on through it to a stile at its far side, then follow a right-hand hedge to cross a stile at the far end of the field. Now bear right through a thicket into a wide hedged lane (bridleway CF11), which leads you to a road at the hamlet of Tower Hill.

Turn right along this road and ignore New Road to your left. Just before the 'Boot', turn left into a lane (path CF12, later CF16) and follow it for a third of a mile until you enter a field. Now follow a right-hand hedge straight on. After a quarter mile, where the hedge turns right, follow it joining path CF14. At a corner of the field, cross a stile and follow a fenced path along the edge of Scatterdells Wood, wiggling to the right and soon reaching Scatterdells Lane. Turn left onto this residential road and follow it to its end. Here go straight on over a stile by a gate onto path CF2 into Scatterdells Wood. At a fork just inside the wood, bear half right, then, where the major path starts to descend and swing to the right, look out for a waymarked path branching left. Fork left onto this and follow it straight on, ignoring a crossing path in a dip and a crossing track beyond it. Now cross a stile and take path KL19, bearing half left across a field to a stile into Barnes Lane. Cross this road and a stile opposite and bear half right, heading towards Shendish House hidden in trees on the next hilltop. On reaching the new A41 fence, turn left and follow it to Rucklers Lane. Turn right onto this road passing under the new A41. After about 120 yards, turn left onto the right-hand of two drives (still path KL19) and follow this uphill through a wood. Where the drive forks, take a narrow path straight on to cross a stile into Shendish Park. Now go straight on across a field to reach a belt of trees concealing Shendish House, then turn right and follow the edge of the tree belt, gradually bearing left to reach a corner of the field.

If wishing to gain a glimpse of the house, go straight on along path KL17 between the trees and a fence, otherwise, turn sharp right onto path KL17, doubling back across the field, with a fine view to your left across the Gade valley including Abbotshill House, now a school, on the other side of the valley, and heading for a gate and stile right of a brick and flint cottage. Cross this stile and take a wide hedged track straight on downhill to cross Rucklers Lane at the bottom. Now follow a right-hand wire-mesh fence straight on uphill through a wood called The Nucket to a stile, then follow a right-hand hedge straight on across a field to a stile leading to Barnes Lane. Cross this road, then go through a hedge gap with a redundant ladder stile opposite and turn immediately left onto a path (still KL17) between the roadside hedge and a school playing field fence. After about 250 yards, turn right, leaving the roadside hedge and continuing to follow the playing field fence for some 350 yards until you emerge at the school entrance. Here turn left onto the school drive, then immediately right into Love Lane and follow it back to your starting point.

WALK 6: Hemel Hempstead Station

Length of Walk: 5.9 miles / 9.5 Km
Starting Point: Forecourt of Hemel Hempstead Station.
Grid Ref: TL043059
Maps: OS Landranger Sheet 166
OS Pathfinder Sheet TL00/10
Chiltern Society FP Maps Nos. 5 & 20

Parking: Hemel Hempstead Station is located just off the old A41 (A4251) at Boxmoor about 1 mile southwest of the town centre. At the mini-roundabout by the station, turn off the main road into Fishery Road, crossing Boxmoor Common and the canal bridge by the 'Fishery Inn',then seek an on-street parking space in one of the side streets.

Notes: At the time of writing, work had not started on the A41 Berkhamsted and King's Langley Bypasses which are due for completion shortly after publication in 1993. Hence the walk description in their vicinity is based only on plans for the new road and so may be somewhat inaccurate. When the new road opens, the old A41 is to be renumbered A4251.

Since the war, Hemel Hempstead, at the confluence of the rivers Gade and Bulbourne, has developed into a large modern town due to its designation in the late 1940s as a 'new town'. Despite this, the surrounding countryside has retained its rural atmosphere and even the town itself is less of a concrete jungle than some of its counterparts, thanks to the preservation of 'green lungs' particularly along the river valleys. Hemel Hempstead also has a long history as its southern part is traversed by a Roman road known as Akeman Street and remains of Roman villas have been found not only here but also in Gadebridge Park to the north of the town centre. In the Middle Ages, Hemel Hempstead must already have been a wealthy market town as is attested by its magnificent twelfth-century church and in the eighteenth and nineteenth centuries, the construction of the Grand Junction Canal, the L&NWR main line to the Midlands and North and several paper mills where modern paper-making methods were pioneered, all to the south of the mediaeval town, caused its expansion southwards.

The walk soon leaves the town behind, climbing the wooded southern slope of the Bulbourne valley to reach Felden and the rural upland plateau beyond, before leading you to Bovingdon Church. The return route then takes you by way of Stoney Lane and the Westbrook Hay gold course with its fine views of the Bulbourne valley, to Bourne End and the Grand Union Canal at Winkwell Swing Bridge, probably the most picturesque location on the Chilterns section of the canal, before following its towpath back to the railway station.

Starting from the main entrance to Hemel Hempstead Station, turn left out of the station past a small car park to cross the old A41 (A4251) just left of a mini-roundabout. Now turn left along its pavement and follow it under a railway bridge and the new A41, then cross the old A41 (A4251) again and take path HH99 following the new A41 embankment to the end of a residential road. Here ignore a house drive ahead and take a parallel hedged path to the left of the drive uphill to a kissing-gate. Go through this, then fork right onto path HH100 climbing through woodland and soon joining a track. Some 15 yards beyond a right-hand bend, fork left onto a path through the woods. On reaching another flinty track (byway HH101), turn right onto it, soon reaching Felden Lane, then turn left onto this road and follow it uphill into Felden.

Where the road bears left by the entrance to Roefields Close, fork half right onto path HH105, a macadam drive leading to Felden Lodge, and follow this through a wood and out onto a golf course. Halfway across the golf course, leave the drive and bear half left to reach a kissing-gate. Go through this and a second kissing-gate then bear half right across a field to pass through a third kissing-gate by a garage right of a house and bungalow. Here cross a drive and follow a left-hand hedge to cross a stile into a field, then follow a right-hand hedge straight on to a kissing-gate into Longcroft Lane.

Turn right onto this road and follow it past a large house called Felden Barns to a sharp left-hand bend. Here leave the road and take path HH112 straight on over a stile and across a field to a hedge gap at the far side of the field. Now on path BV16, bear half right across a second field to join the edge of Bury Wood by a clump of trees in the field concealing a pond.Bear slightly left here and follow the outside edge of the wood, later a right-hand hedge, straight on through two fields to cross a stile at the far end of the second field. Now turn right and follow the right-hand hedge around a field corner and then straight on along the edge of a prairie field for over half a mule to cross a stile at the far end of the field. Here bear half right onto path

BV17 across a field towards Bovingdon Church to a stile, then continue straight on to a white-painted stile between a bungalow and an electricity sub-station. Cross this and a further stile to reach Church Street, Bovingdon opposite the church.

Set in one of the largest churchyards in Hertfordshire, Bovingdon Church was rebuilt in 1845 on the site of a thirteenth-century predecessor, from which the effigy of a knight dating from around 1400 is preserved. The village to your left has some attractive old cottages, but has been rather swamped by modern development.

Fork right onto the road passing the church, then at a sharp left-hand bend, turn right onto byway BV20, a rough lane called Stoney Lane, following it straight on for half a mile until you reach a number of houses. By a right-hand house with lattice windows called Huntsmoor, turn left onto a macadam residential road and follow it out to the B4505.

Turn right onto this road, passing a brick-and-flint lodge to your left. Just past this lodge, cross the road and take a macadam drive opposite (path BV23), turning immediately right over a stile by a gate. Now follow the obvious path straight on through Gorsefield Wood, eventually emerging onto a macadam golf club road. Turn right onto this road following it past the car park and the clubhouse, then bearing left to reach some former farm buildings. By these buildings, the road turns right and where it ends, take a grassy track (still path BV23) straight on, with fine views ahead across the Bulbourne valley with Berkhamsted to your left and the edge of Hemel Hempstead to your right. Go straight on past a bungalow and just past a left-hand seat, by a large oak bush, turn left, passing just right of a clump of trees with the fourteenth green to your right. Also to your right is an imposing early nineteenth-century manor house called Westbrook Hay which, at one time, housed the offices of the Hemel Hempstead New Town Development Corporation. Now continue straight on downhill to cross a bridge over the new A41, soon joining a left-hand hedge and following it to cross a stile by a gate into a green lane (byway HH115). Here take the green lane straight on to the old A41 (A4251) at Bourne End.

Cross this road and turn right onto its pavement. After some 350 yards, just before a petrol station, turn left down a narrow lane called Winkwell, soon crossing a narrow bridge over the River Bulbourne. On reaching the Winkwell Swing Bridge over the Grand Union Canal, opposite the picturesque sixteenth-century 'Three Horseshoes', turn right onto the canal towpath. Now follow the towpath in its deceptively rural setting frequented by ducks and fishermen, for just over a mile, passing under a railway bridge and later a small road bridge. On reaching a second road bridge by the 'Fishery Inn', climb a

WALK 6

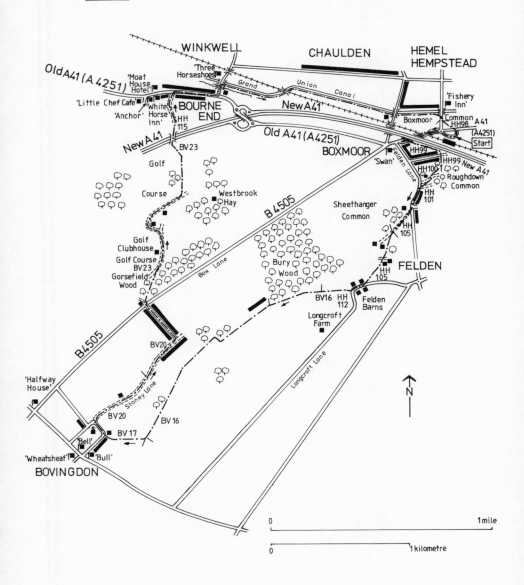

shallow flight of steps to Fishery Road, then turn right and almost immediately left, crossing the road and passing through a kissing-gate. Now take macadam path HH98 across Boxmoor Common to a second kissing-gate and a pelican crossing on the old A41 (A4251) where the railway station is in front of you.

WALK 7: Berkhamsted (North)

Length of Walk: (A) 7.9 miles / 12.7 Km
                      (B) 2.3 miles / 3.7 Km
                      (C) 5.2 miles / 8.3 Km

Starting Point: (A/B) Road junction by northern entrance
                              to Berkhamsted Railway Station.
                      (C) Potten End Village Hall.

Grid Ref: (A/B)   SP994082
                (C)   TL016089

Maps: OS Landranger Sheets 165 (A/B only) & 166 (all)
          OS Pathfinder Sheets SP80/90 (A/B only),
                  TL00/10 (all) & TL01/11 (A/C only)
          Chiltern Society FP Map No. 20 (all) or No. 17 (B only).

How to get there / Parking: (A/B) From the junction of the
    old A41 (A4251) and A416 in Berkhamsted town centre,
take the Potten End road and park either in the car park
on the left or at the railway station.
(C) Potten End. 1.8 miles northeast of Berkhamsted, may
be reached from the town by taking one of several
signposted routes. On reaching the village green, ignore
two turnings to the right and park in a small car park on
your right opposite the village hall.

Notes: The old A41 is to be renumbered A4251 in 1993 when
the A41 Berkhamsted Bypass is opened. Heavy nettle
growth may be encountered in summer particularly on
path GG68 on Walks A and C.

Berkhamsted, with its centre in the bottom of a steep-sided river valley, is, in many ways, a typical Chiltern town as it has spread first along its valley and later up the hills on either side. Nevertheless its history sets it apart from its neighbours. In 1066, William the Conqueror, following his victory at the Battle of Hastings, passed through the town on his circuitous approach to London and here accepted the surrender of the Saxon nobles. Shortly after this, he gave the manor to his half-brother, Robert of Mortain who built a castle in this strategically important defile through the Chilterns as a way of protecting London from possible attack. This castle was later destroyed and was rebuilt by the famous Archbishop of

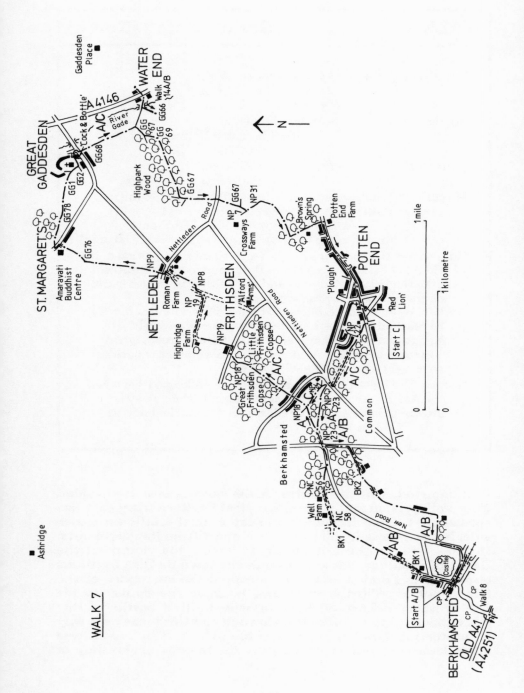

WALK 7

42

Canterbury, Thomas à Becket. The ruins of this castle, which was last occupied in 1496, can still be seen today near the railway station. Amongst the prominent names linked with the castle are the Black Prince who lived in it as Duke of Cornwall, King John of France who was imprisoned there in 1361 and the poet, Geoffrey Chaucer who was at one time its Clerk of Works. Another poet associated with the town is William Cowper, born the son of its rector in 1731, and monuments both to him and his mother are to be found in the thirteenth-century parish church, one of the largest in Hertfordshire.

Walks A and B lead you from the town to its extensive heathy and wooded common returning with fine views over the town, while Walks A and C explore the quiet ridges and valleys beyond with their small picturesque villages and scenic views.

Starting from the road junction by the northern entrance to Berkhamsted railway station, **Walks A and B** take Brownlow Road northwards past the ruins of Berkhamsted Castle. At a right-hand bend, fork left onto Castle Hill and follow this road straight on uphill. At a left-hand bend by the entrance to Berkhamsted Cricket Club, leave the road and take path BK1 straight on over a stile into the Wellcome Foundation car park, then follow a private road straight on to a second car park. Now take a grassy track straight on beside a powerline to a gate and stile, then follow a left-hand fence straight on to a double stile at the far side of the field. Cross the right-hand part of this stile and follow a left-hand hedge straight on through three fields to a stile leading to a track junction at Well Farm. Here turn right onto the right-hand track (path NC58), passing right of the farm buildings, then climbing to join a macadam drive by a bungalow. Where this drive bears right, leave it and go straight on over a stile onto Berkhamsted Common. Now take the obvious scrubland path NC56 straight on uphill to meet New Road.

Turn left onto this road and follow it uphill to a T-junction near a war memorial, where those wishing to take **Walk B** should turn right onto the Potten End and Water End road and then read the last paragraph. **Walk A** crosses the major road and takes bridleway NP23 straight on, passing right of the war memorial and crossing a golf fairway. In the next tree belt, look out for a signposted fork to the left. Fork left onto this defined path and follow it straight on across a fairway, through a tree belt and across another fairway to reach signposted path NP18 between garden hedges.

Walks A and C follow this path to cross a residential road, then take a fenced path straight on. On entering Great Frithsden Copse, disregard a crossing path and go straight on for some 400 yards. Where another path merges from your right, bear slightly left and continue downhill to a road at the scattered hamlet of Frithsden (pronounced 'Freezeden').

Turn right onto this road passing two houses, then after about 80 yards turn left over a stile in a wall under a tree onto fenced path NP19 and follow it to a stile. Cross this and follow a right-hand hedge uphill. On reaching a barbed-wire fence near Highridge Farm, cross a stile a few yards to your right and follow a fenced path past the farm to a stile leading to a stony track on the ridgetop, where Ashridge House, rebuilt for the seventh Earl of Bridgewater by Wyatt in the early nineteenth century, comes into view on a hill to your left. Turn right onto this track and follow it through two fields. On reaching double gates, turn left to cross a further stile leading to a rough road known locally as 'Roman Road'.

Now ignore a stile to your left and turn left onto the rough road. Where it starts to descend into a walled cutting constructed for the canal-building third Duke of Bridgewater, fork right through a squeeze-stile by a gate onto path NP8 turning left over a stile into a belt of trees. Now follow this path downhill through the tree belt beside the sunken way, passing through two squeeze-stiles by an old bridge over the sunken way and continuing downhill to reach a flight of steps descending to rejoin the road. Now follow this downhill into Nettleden, a tiny village with picturesque seventeenth-century cottages and a church rebuilt in brick in 1811 but retaining its fifteenth-century tower.

At a T-junction, turn left onto a road passing double gates, then turn right through an anti-horse barrier onto path NP9, following a right-hand hedge uphill through two fields with a left-hand hedge enclosing the path in places. Now cross a stile and take path GG76 following a right-hand hedge through a field containing Buddhist shrines. At the far side of this field, keep right of a group of young trees to enter a fenced path which joins a gravel drive and leads to to a road at St. Margaret's, named after the former twelfth-century nunnery of St. Margaret de Bosco.

Turn left onto this road, then, after about 50 yards, turn right over a concealed stile by a gate onto path GG78. Now bear slightly left, following the outside edge of St. Margaret's Copse downhill to a stile. Here leave the wood and go straight on across a field, passing right of a clump of hawthorn bushes, then bearing slightly left to reach a hedge gap by a twin-poled electricity pylon. Go through this gap and take path GG1, bearing half right across a field to a stile right of a long line of concrete garages at Great Gaddesden. Do not cross this stile, but bear half right onto path GG2, following the churchyard wall beneath a row of lime trees. At the far end of the churchyard, turn left over a stile into it and follow a right-hand wall through the churchyard to a lychgate.

Great Gaddesden's twelfth-century church with its massive fifteenth-century tower decorated with gargoyles is notable for the Roman bricks used in its construction, which are believed to have derived from a Roman villa on the same site, and the early Georgian Halsey mausoleum containing more than twenty monuments.

Now go through the lychgate and take a road, bearing right and ignoring a turning to the left. At a T-junction by the 'Cock and Bottle', turn right, then immediately left onto fenced path GG68 leading to a stile.Now continue between hedges to cross a further stile, then follow a left-hand hedge straight on across a field to a stile at its far end. Cross this, then turn right over a second stile onto fenced path GG67, following it uphill into Highpark Wood. Just inside the wood, turn left onto path GG69 and follow it along the inside edge of the wood for nearly half a mile with views to your left at first across Water End in the Gade valley towards Gaddesden Place on the hill opposite, built by Wyatt for the Halseys in 1768–1773 and still their home today. On reaching a T-junction of paths, turn left onto path GG67, soon crossing a stile into a field with a view across the valley towards Potten End on the next ridge. Now go straight on downhill heading for the corner of a hedge on the hillside opposite to reach a stile onto Nettleden Road.

Cross this road and a stile opposite, then go straight on, now heading for the near corner of a wood called Brown's Spring and ignoring a branching path to your left (where you join path NP7) to reach a marker post. Now turn left onto path NP31 to the corner of a hedge where you turn right and follow the nearside of the hedge to a stile in a corner of the field, then go straight on, soon entering the wood and following its inside edge to a stile. Cross this and follow an enclosed path uphill ignoring a branching path to your right, soon passing gardens and crossing a stile and eventually reaching Water End Road on the edge of Potten End. Turn right onto its pavement and follow the major road straight on for half a mile, ignoring all side turnings, to reach the village hall.

From Potten End village hall, where **Walk C** starts, **Walks A and C** follow the Berkhamsted road to the edge of the village green, then opposite the turning to Bourne End, turn right onto bridleway NP22 following a gravel drive towards a house called 'Bryher'. About 25 yards short of its gate, turn left onto a path following the inside edge of the wood and ignoring all branching and crossing paths. On reaching a sunken gully, part of the ancient earthwork known as Grim's Ditch, enter it and follow it straight on for a quarter mile, crossing a golf course at one point, to reach Nettleden Road. Turn right onto this road, then almost immediately left. Now **Walk C** takes the right-hand of two bridleways (NP24) straight on, ignoring all lesser branching paths. On emerging onto the golf course, bear slightly left, following an obvious path passing left of the 16th tee and right of the 15th green and heading towards a prominent birch tree on the edge of the wood ahead. Just before reaching this tree, turn right onto signposted path NP18 between garden hedges. Now go back to the bottom of page 43.

Walk A takes the left-hand of the two bridleways (NP23) and follows its winding course through woodland, ignoring lesser branching paths and soon reaching a fairway. Go straight on across this into further woodland. Here keep right at a fork, then go straight on, crossing two further fairways to pass left of the war memorial and reach a road junction where you turn left onto the Potten End and Water End road.

Walks A and B now follow this road to the entrance to Berkhamsted Golf Club, then turn right onto it. Where the macadam road turns left, leave it and take a rough road straight on. At the end of the road by the gate of 'Fairhill', bear half right onto path BK2 into woodland, keeping left at a fork and following a garden wall to a stile. Cross this and a second stile with a superb view across Berkhamsted beginning to open out ahead, then follow a left-hand fence to a stile by a gated cattle grid. Now take a concrete road to cross another stile by a cattle grid, then follow the left-hand hedge generally straight on through three fields. At the far end of the third field, turn right and follow a left-hand hedge, later a line of beech trees downhill to a stile onto New Road opposite the ruins of Berkhamsted Castle. Cross the road, then turn left onto its pavement and follow it to a crossroads. Here fork right into a road called White Hill and follow it beside the railway back to Berkhamsted Station.

Length of Walk: 8.3 miles / 13.3 Km

Starting Point: Junction of old A41 (A4251) (High Street) and A416 (Kings Road), Berkhamsted.

Grid Ref: SP991079

Maps: OS Landranger Sheet 165
OS Pathfinder Sheet SP80/90
Chiltern Society FP Maps Nos. 8 & 17

Parking: There are several public car parks in the centre of Berkhamsted.

Notes: At the time of writing, work had not started on the A41 Berkhamsted Bypass which is due for completion shortly after publication in 1993. The walk description in its vicinity is therefore only based on plans for the new road and so may be somewhat inaccurate. When the new road opens, the old A41 is to be renumbered A4251. Heavy nettle growth may be found in summer on bridleway AG2 and path BK46.

Berkhamsted, the name of which is locally pronounced 'Berk'msted' and has, till quite recently, been prone to a number of variations in spelling, is described in the introduction to Walk 7.

The walk takes you westwards uphill through leafy suburbs to cross the bypass and continue by way of the lost village of Marlin to the hilltop Buckinghamshire village of Hawridge with its moated manor house. From here, it takes you south-eastwards along the crest of a ridge and then down into Chesham Vale before returning by way of Ashley Green and Hockeridge Wood to Berkhamsted.

Starting from the junction of the old A41 (A4251) (High Street) and the A416 (Kings Road), take Kings Road uphill. After some 200 yards, turn right into Charles Street, then take the second turning left, Doctors Commons Road. Opposite No. 19, turn right into a fenced alleyway (path BK14). Follow this straight on, joining a right-hand road for a few yards and then leaving it again, crossing a drive and eventually emerging into North Road. Turn left into this road, then immediately right into Anglefield Road and after about 25 yards, fork

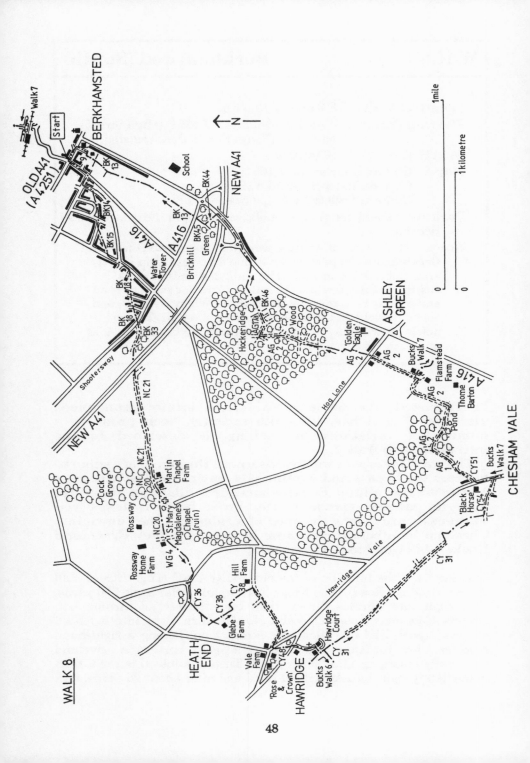

WALK 8

48

left onto path BK15, an alleyway left of a double garage and follow it straight on to reach a narrow lane without pavements. Turn left into this lane and ignore first a left-hand turn, then a right-hand turn called Greystoke Close. Opposite a house called 'Chilterns', turn right onto path BK18, a fenced alleyway by the entrance to 'Little Corner' and follow it straight on, crossing another alley and two roads and eventually emerging onto a third road at the edge of the town.

Turn right onto this road, then immediately left into a rough lane (path BK33) and follow it downhill. At the bottom, on entering a field, follow a left-hand hedge straight on to a stile onto the bypass. Cross the bypass and a stile opposite, then join bridleway NC21 following a rough track straight on beside a left-hand hedge. Where the track passes through a hedge gap into another field, continue to follow it straight on, now with a hedge to your right. Near the far end of this field, follow the track reverting to the other side of the hedge. Now take bridleway NC20, a wide grassy lane, straight on, keeping left of a wood called Cock Grove and passing Marlin Chapel Farm, where there are traces of a moat and it would appear that there might once have been a village.

Where the lane opens out into a field, leave the track, bearing slightly right and passing right of the ruins of St. Mary Magdalene's Chapel (already a ruin in 1822) to a gate and stile into Rossway Park with a view of Rossway House ahead. Now go straight on across the park, gradually diverging from a left-hand fence to reach a stile left of a bungalow on the far side of the park. Cross this stile and a rough lane and take path WG4 straight on through a hedge gap, following a right-hand hedge downhill to a stile in the valley bottom. Cross this and turn right onto a road following the Buckinghamshire boundary; then at a fork, bear left onto the road signposted to Wigginton and Tring. Just past a right-hand copse, turn left through a gap in the roadside bank onto bridleway CY36, following the left-hand side of a strip of grass, later a hedge uphill to reach a gate. Do not go through this gate, but instead turn left onto path CY38 and follow a right-hand hedge to a stile at the far end of the field. Cross this stile, then turn left and follow a left-hand hedge to a field corner. Here turn right and continue to follow the left-hand hedge through two fields to a stile into a rough lane near Hill Farm.

Turn right into the lane and follow it downhill, bearing right at the bottom to reach a road junction by Vale Farm on the edge of Hawridge Common. Turn sharp left onto the road, then immediately fork right opposite a rusty white gate onto path CY48, climbing across the wooded common to emerge onto a road at the top of the hill opposite Church Lane. Cross this road and take Church Lane straight on to reach Hawridge Church with its green-painted bellcote, built in 1856 on the site of its thirteenth-century predecessor, and Hawridge Court, a timber-framed manor house with a partially filled moat.

By the entrance to Hawridge Court, turn right onto path CY39, a narrow alleyway between a hedge and a cottage, to reach a stile into a field where the moat is visible to your left. In the field, turn left onto path CY31, briefly joining Bucks Walk 6. Now cross a stile by a gate in the corner of the field and go straight on across the next field to a stile at the far side. Cross this and follow a grassy track straight on along the crest of the ridge through two large fields with fine views of Hawridge Vale to your left, a Victorian house called Thorne Barton on a hilltop near Ashley Green ahead and the outskirts of Chesham further to the right. After nearly three-quarters of a mile, at the far end of the second field, go through a hedge gap then turn left and follow the left-hand hedge downhill to a corner of the field. Here turn right and continue to follow a left-hand hedge to the bottom corner of the field. Now turn left over a stile onto path CY54, a grassy hedged lane, and follow it straight on for over 300 yards, with the right-hand hedge later giving way to a fence, to reach a gate and stile leading to the road in Chesham Vale.

Turn left onto this road joining Bucks Walk 7. Opposite the 'Black Horse' turn right onto bridleway CY51 (later AG1), a flinty sunken lane, and follow it straight on for a quarter mile. Where the lane forks and the left-hand option goes straight on to a gate into a wood, turn right onto bridleway AG2; then, where the main track turns right again through large green gates, leave it and take a narrower sunken track straight on, climbing gradually through a copse and past a pond. At the top of the hill, follow the lane bearing left and continuing between hedges for some 300 yards until you reach the end of a concrete farm road. Go straight on along this, swinging right to reach Flamstead Farm. Here turn left (still on AG2) and leaving Bucks Walk 7, pass left of a Dutch barn to a gate into another hedged lane, which you follow for a quarter mile to reach a road called Hog Lane on the edge of Ashley Green.

Cross this road and take a fenced path (still AG2) straight on to a stile into a field, then follow a left-hand hedge straight on to the corner of the field. Here transfer through a gap in the left-hand hedge to its other side and follow it downhill, turning left then right at one point, to reach a stile into Hockeridge Wood. Having crossed this, ignore a crossing path and take a woodland track straight on for a third of a mile, disregarding a crossing track by a picnic table. On passing a small picnic area to your right with three tables, turn right onto path AG17a, a flinty track and follow this downhill, ignoring three right-hand forking tracks, to reach a crossing track at the bottom marking the county boundary. Cross this and take path BK46 straight on uphill. Near a right-hand bungalow, where the path turns left, leave it bearing right to cross a stile out of the wood. Now follow the outside edge of the wood straight on to a corner of the wood, then bear half right across the field to white gates leading to the A416.

Turn left onto this road and follow it to a new roundabout. Here take the A416 straight on to cross a bridge over the bypass. At the far end of the bridge, turn left onto path BK44 and follow it through woodland known as Brickhill Green. At the far side of the wood, turn right onto path BK45 and follow it along the inside edge of the wood to the A416. Cross this main road bearing slightly left and take path BK13 through a fence gap with an old kissing-gate frame. Now follow a line of trees straight on across a school playing field with views across Berkhamsted to the hills beyond. At the far side, take an alleyway straight on downhill, soon passing a field to your right, to reach another school playing field. Go straight on across this playing field to an alleyway left of a school, then follow the alleyway (path BK9) straight on, soon turning right to reach the end of a cul-de-sac street. Turn left to reach the High Street, then left again for your starting point.

WALK 9: Northchurch Common

Length of Walk: 6.9 miles / 11.2 Km

Starting Point: Informal car park at bend in B4506 half a mile north of Northchurch.

Grid Ref: SP979095

Maps: OS Landranger Sheet 165
OS Pathfinder Sheets SP80/90 & SP81/91
Chiltern Society FP Maps Nos. 17 & 19

How to get there / Parking: Northchurch Common, 1.5 miles northwest of Berkhamsted, may be reached from the town by taking the A41 (A4251) northwestwards to Northchurch, then turning right onto the B4506 and following it for half a mile to a sharp left-hand bend. Here ignore a turning to the right, then almost immediately turn right into a grassy car park.

Notes: The old A41 is to be renumbered A4251 in 1993 when the A41 Berkhamsted Bypass opens.

Northchurch Common on the hill above Northchurch is one of a belt of largely wooded commons stretching from the outskirts of Berkhamsted to Aldbury and Ivinghoe Beacon now managed by the National Trust. The village in the Bulbourne valley below, which you skirt early in the walk, is today little more than a suburb of nearby Berkhamsted, but it was once more important than its urban neighbour. In Roman times Northchurch was the site of a small town and in Saxon times it had a castle and a stone-built church, part of which is incorporated in the present largely thirteenth-century building. In the church is a brass memorial to Peter the Wildboy who became famous in 1725 after being found living wild in the woods near Hamelin in King George I's country of birth and joint kingdom, the Electorate of Hanover. Peter was brought to England by the King, but, when it proved impossible to educate him, he was sent to a farm in Northchurch where he spent the rest of his left and was buried in 1785. In more modern times, although the relative importance of Northchurch has declined, its location on various major transport routes through the Chilterns has caused it to grow and develop into a commuter dormitory.

The walks first leads you down towards Northchurch to join

the Grand Union Canal towpath and follow it for over a mile to Cow Roast Lock. Having left the canal, you walk over a hill to the picturesque village of Aldbury before climbing the wooded escarpment to reach the Bridgewater Monument. From here the walk returns by way of Aldbury's wooden common, with a fine view of Tring and the Vale of Aylesbury, and Northchurch Common with its mixture of open grassland and heathland to your starting point.

Starting from the entrance to the car park, turn left onto the B4506 and follow it downhill towards Northchurch for nearly half a mile to the bridge over the Grand Union Canal on the edge of the village. Having crossed this bridge, turn right through a gate onto the canal towpath at Northchurch Lock. Follow this pleasant waterside path northwestwards for three-quarters of a mile to a road bridge at Dudswell. Turn right over this bridge, then immediately left rejoining the towpath at Dudswell Lock and following it for over half a mile to bridge no. 137 at Cow Roast Lock, the name of which is thought to be a corruption of 'Cow Rest' as the nearby 'Cow Roast Inn' may have been a resting place for cattle drovers on their way down the modern A41 (A4251) to the London markets.

Pass under the bridge, climb a flight of steps to the lock, then turn sharp right between walls to reach Wharf Lane. Turn left onto this road and follow it for about 150 yards, then turn left over a stile onto path NC29 and go straight across a field to an ungainly footbridge over the railway. Having crossed this bridge, keep straight on across the next field to a gap in a fenced hedge. Go through this gap then turn right onto a fenced farm track, soon turning left and passing the farmhouse at Norcott Court Farm.

On reaching the farm drive, turn left onto it then cross a stile by a gate and turn right, keeping right of farm buildings to cross a stile by a gate. Still on NC29 bear half left, crossing the field diagonally with fine views across the Bulbourne valley to your left and behind you, to cross a stile by a gate in the far corner. Here take a grassy track to the corner of a right-hand tree belt then bear slightly left across the field to the corner of a hedge. Follow this hedge straight on to a corner of the field then turn right through a hedge gap and belt of trees to a stile. Here take path AB3 bearing half left across a field to a stile in the top left-hand corner where a fine view opens out through the Tring Gap to Pitstone cement works and the Aylesbury Vale beyond. Cross this stile and follow the edge of a right-hand wood called The Hangings straight on, ignoring a crossing bridleway. At the corner of the wood turn right, following the edge of the wood for a further 200 yards, with a fine view ahead of Aldbury hidden in trees backed by

Clipper Down, then cross a stile by a gate into a hedged lane and follow it along the edge of the wood to a stile by a gate at the far end. Now bear half left across a field, with the top of the Bridgewater Monument visible over the treetops to your right, to cross a stile in the far corner of the field. Here follow a right-hand hedge past a copse then cross another stile and go straight on across a further field to a stile leading onto Newground Road.

Turn left onto this road, then at a left-hand bend, just before a concrete drive, turn right through a hedge gap onto path AB68 and bear half right across a field to the corner of a hedge. Here bear half right again and follow the right hand hedge to cross a stile at the far end of the field. Now follow a left-hand hedge straight on to cross a further stile into a hedged path. Take this path to reach the end of a village street in Aldbury, then follow this street straight on past the 'Valiant Trooper' to the picturesque village green with its pond, ancient stocks, seventeenth-century manor house and a number of attractive cottages.

Joining the reverse direction of Walk 12 take Stocks Road straight on past the green and the 'Greyhound' and out of the village. Some 200 yards beyond its last cottage, having rounded a left-hand bend, turn right onto path AB33 up some steps, through a hedge gap and over a stile and follow a left-hand hedge uphill for some 50 yards until you reach a stile in it. Cross this then (leaving Walk 12 again) take path AB32 bearing half right across a field to a stile into a wood some distance to the right of an imposing house on the hillside called Little Stocks. Inside the wood take a path straight on, ignoring two crossing paths and climbing steeply to reach a T-junction of paths near a cottage. Here turn right onto bridleway AB29 keeping right at a fork and soon entering a small clearing. At the far side of the clearing bear slightly left, disregarding a crossing bridleway and continuing through beechwoods to emerge in a clearing by the Bridgewater Monument, erected in 1832 in memory of the third Duke of Bridgewater (1736–1803), 'the Father of the English canal system'. This monument stands at the end of a 1.5-mile-long avenue known as Prince's Riding which was laid out in about 1760 as part of Ashridge Park and the house, rebuilt by James Wyatt and Sir Jeffry Wyatville between 1803 and 1820, can just be seen at the other end.

By the monument turn right along the edge of the clearing to join a stony track (bridleway AB20). Bear slightly right onto this, re-entering the woods, ignoring a lesser fork to the left and passing through a clearing planted with young trees with a fine view ahead across Aldbury towards Tring. On entering mature woodland, ignore a branching bridleway to the right and a crossing path, then at a fork go right onto bridleway AB26, a sunken track dropping through

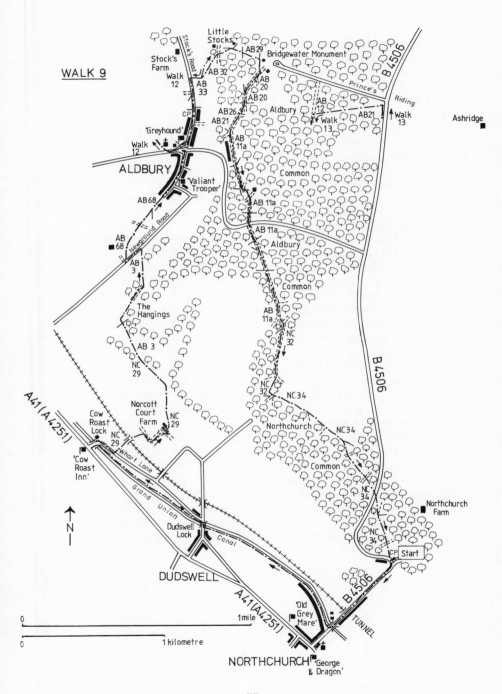

WALK 9

Stock's Farm
Stocks Road
Little Stocks
Walk 12
AB 33
AB 32
AB 29
Bridgewater Monument
Prince's
Riding
B4506
CP
'Greyhound'
Walk 12
AB 32
AB 20
AB 20
AB26
AB 21
Aldbury
AB 12
AB21
Walk 13
Walk 13
Ashridge
ALDBURY
AB 11a
'Valiant Trooper'
Common
AB68
Newground Road
AB 11a
AB 68
AB 11a
Aldbury
AB 3
Common
The Hangings
AB 11a
NC 32
AB 3
NC 29
NC 32
A41(A4251)
Cow Roast Lock
Norcott Court Farm
NC 29
NC 29
NC 32
NC 34
NC 34
Northchurch
'Cow Roast Inn'
Wharf Lane
Grand Union
Common
Northchurch Farm
N
Dudswell Lock
Canal
NC 34
NC 34
DUDSWELL
A41(A4251)
CP Start
B4506
'Old Grey Mare'
TUNNEL
0   1 mile
0   1 kilometre
NORTHCHURCH 'George & Dragon'

55

beechwoods towards Aldbury. After about 150 yards join bridleway AB21 which merges from your left, then after a further 50 yards, at a path junction with a steep chalk face to your left, bear half left onto bridleway AB11a, a gently rising sunken path which soon enters an ancient yew wood, now with a fence to your right. Where a path commences on top of the right-hand bank of the gully, take this path, keeping parallel to the gully and ignoring a crossing path. Eventually this path leads you to a clearing with a bench and a fine view of Tring and the Vale of Aylesbury. At the far end of the clearing turn left and follow a track beneath a power line. By a pylon with a grey box attached to it, turn right onto a well-used bridleway into the trees (still AB11a). On reaching a rough drive, continue straight across it and ignore all other crossing tracks until you reach the macadam road across Aldbury Common.

Cross this road and take well-used bridleway AB11a straight on for a quarter mile ignoring all crossing paths until a field comes into view to your right. Now go straight on for a further quarter mile to reach a fork by a corner of the right-hand field. Here keep left then at a second fork go right onto bridleway NC32 which soon bears left into an area of bracken on Northchurch Common. Soon the bracken to your left gives way to open grassland and Berkhamsted comes into view ahead. On reaching another area of wooded common, ignore crossing tracks and go straight on into the wooded area. At a six-way junction by the corner of more grassland bear half left onto bridleway NC34 and follow it straight on along the edge of this grassland for over a third of a mile, passing through a dip where Northchurch can be seen to your right and reaching another rise. About 100 yards before the far end of the grassland, by a group of young silver birch trees, turn right onto a mown grassy track through the bracken (still NC34) and follow it downhill ignoring all crossing tracks. After crossing a flint track, you start climbing again and soon reach the B4506. Cross this road and take bridleway NC34 straight on over the top of a hill, ignoring a branching bridleway to your left and descending to reach scrubland. Where the mown path turns left, leave it and take a narrower path straight on into the bushes, crossing a macadam drive and eventually reaching the grassy clearing by the B4506 at your starting point.

WALK 10: Tring

Length of Walk: 6.8 miles / 11.0 Km

Starting Point: 'Rose and Crown Hotel', Tring.

Grid Ref: SP925114

Maps: OS Landranger Sheet 165
OS Pathfinder Sheets SP80/90 & SP81/91
Chiltern Society FP Map No. 18

Parking: Public car park on the north side of Tring High Street (A4251 – shortly to be renumbered as a 'B' road), just east of Tring Church.

Notes: Heavy nettle growth may be encountered in places in summer months.

Tring, situated at a gap in the Chiltern escarpment, has always been a place of some importance as it straddles Akeman Street, a Roman road from London to Cirencester, near its junction with the Ancient British Upper Icknield Way which itself passes through the suburbs of the town. In more modern times Tring has also found itself on the routes of various generations of main traffic arteries in the form of the A41 trunk road from London to Aylesbury and Birmingham, the Grand Union Canal from London to the Midlands and the London Midland main railway from Euston to Birmingham and the North. The town boasts a principally fifteenth-century church with a Grinling Gibbons monument to Sir William Gore dating from 1707. Not far from the town centre is a large mansion called Tring Park which was originally designed by Sir Christopher Wren. This house, reputedly often visited in its early years by Nell Gwynne, was for two centuries the home of the family of Sir William Gore, the first Director of the Bank of England. It was later acquired by the Rothschilds who enlarged the house giving it its Victorian appearance. The surrounding park, once noted for its tranquillity, was desecrated in the 1970s by the building of the Tring Bypass which severs the house from the bulk of the park, but if one can ignore the traffic, it remains a place of beauty.

The walk takes you from Tring through Tring Park and across the bypass, then climbs the wooded escarpment to join

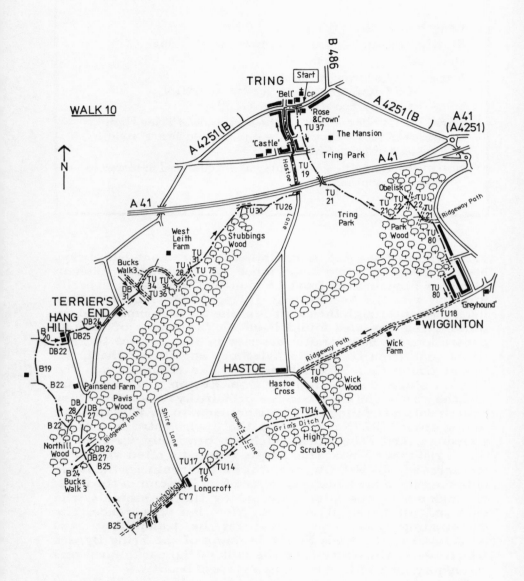

WALK 10

TRING

Start

B 486

'Bell'   CP

A 4251 (B)

A 4251 (B)   A 41 (A4251)

'Rose & Crown'

TU 37

The Mansion

N

'Castle'

Hastoe Lane

Tring Park

A 41

TU 19

TU 21

Obelisk

Ridgeway Path

TU 22   TU

TU 21

TU 21

A 41

West Leith Farm

TU 30   TU 26

Stubbings Wood

Tring Park

Park Wood

TU 80

Bucks Walk3

TU 31

TU 28   TU 75

TU 34 34   DB 31   TU 36

TU 80

'Greyhound'

TU 18

TERRIER'S END

DB 24

WIGGINTON

HANG HILL

B 20   DB 25

DB 22

Wick Farm

B 19

Ridgeway Path

B 22

HASTOE

Painsend Farm

Hastoe Cross

Wick Wood

DB 28   DB 27

Pavis Wood

TU 18

B 22

Shire Lane

Ridgeway Path

TU 14

Grims Ditch

High Scrubs

Northill Wood

DB 29   DB 27

B 25

Brown's Lane

B 24   Bucks Walk 3

TU 17

TU 14

TU 16

Grims Ditch

Longcroft

CY 7

CY 7

B 25

0	1mile

0	1 kilometre

the Ridgeway Path near Wigginton. From here it follows first the Ridgeway Path and later an ancient earthwork known as Grim's Ditch across the plateau into Buckinghamshire before descending through beechwoods to the isolated hamlet of Hang Hill and returning to Tring.

Starting from the 'Rose and Crown Hotel' opposite Tring Church, take the High Street westwards for about 50 yards. Just before a zebra crossing, turn left into a narrow alleyway (path TU37). At a T-junction of paths, turn left, soon turning right again to resume your previous direction, then go straight on to reach Park Street opposite one of the lodges of Tring Park. Cross this road bearing slightly right and take fenced macadam path TU19 to a spiralled footbridge over the A41 into Tring Park. At the far end of the bridge, go through a kissing-gate onto fenced path TU21 following the bypass fence straight on, then after a few yards, bearing half right across the outer part of the park, with views over your left shoulder of Tring Park House. On crossing a stile by a gate to enter Park Wood, follow a flint track (path TU22) uphill through the woods to an obelisk. Legend has it that this obelisk was erected by Charles II in memory of Nell Gwynne, but as he died first, this seems unlikely.

Just before the obelisk, turn right, crossing another track and taking a narrower path (still TU22) steeply uphill. At the top at a junction of tracks and paths, bear half left onto path TU21, a track alongside a plantation, soon reaching a gate and handgate by a house. Go through the handgate, then turn right over a stile onto path TU80, the Ridgeway Path. Now follow a left-hand hedge straight on along the edge of the plantation, ignoring branching paths to the right and garden entrances to the left and at one point passing through a squeeze-stile. On reaching a crossing macadam drive, go straight on, still following a left-hand hedge through woodland which later gives way to scrub, until you come to a garden gate in front of you. Here turn right and follow the garden hedge to a stile, then turn left onto a fenced path leading to a stile at the far end of the adjoining field into a stony lane near the end of a village street at Wigginton.

Turn right into this lane (path TU18/Ridgeway Path) and follow it across the upland plateau for over three-quarters of a mile, passing Wick Farm and eventually reaching a macadam road near a road junction at Hastoe, the highest village in Hertfordshire. Turn left onto this road (leaving the Ridgeway Path) and follow it for a quarter mile. Where a left-hand wood ends and a right-hand wood called High Scrubs begins, turn right over a stile into High Scrubs and bear slightly right onto TU14, the right-hand of two woodland paths. This path follows Grim's Ditch, an ancient earthwork of unknown origin clearly visible to your right, straight on through the wood for a quarter mile, then goes straight across a field to a hedge gap ahead. Here cross a rough lane called Brown's Lane and go straight on through another hedge gap. Now follow the left side of a belt of trees concealing Grim's Ditch to the far end of the field. Here turn right onto path TU16 through the tree belt crossing Grim's Ditch. On entering another field, go straight on for a few yards to the beginning of another tree belt, then turn left through a hedge gap onto path TU17 following a left-hand hedge to a stile and gate onto a road called Shire Lane which forms the boundary between Hertfordshire and Buckinghamshire.

Turn left onto this road and after some 60 yards, opposite Longcroft farmhouse, turn right onto bridleway CY7, a macadam farm road. Take this straight on for a third of a mile passing a few houses and some farm buildings in a hollow. At the top of the next rise, turn right over a stile opposite a handgate onto path B25 and go straight across a large arable field to enter the distant Pavis Wood near where a hedge to the right reaches it. Inside the wood take path DB27 generally straight on, soon crossing the heavily-used Ridgeway Path and following a defined path downhill through a plantation. On entering mature woodland, the path joins a sunken gully and follows it downhill through the wood to the valley bottom.

At the bottom of the hill, by a Buckinghamshire County Council noticeboard, turn sharp left onto path DB28 following the inside edge of the wood along the valley bottom. On reaching a clearing with another County Council noticeboard to your left, fork right, soon turning right again onto hedged path B22. Take this path straight on for a quarter mile. Where it starts to swing perceptibly to the left and a house becomes visible through the trees ahead, turn right onto path B19 passing through a hedge gap into a field. Now follow the left-hand field edge straight on to the far end of the field. Here turn sharp right onto path B20, crossing the field diagonally to a gap between the corner of a fence and the end of a hedge. Go though this gap and take path DB22 following the left-hand fence past some attractive thatched cottages to cross a stile in the corner of the field, then descend through a hedge gap into a narrow road at Hang Hill.

Turn left along this road passing the thatched cottages. Opposite Hang Hill Cottage, turn right through a gate onto path DB25 following a right-hand hedge to the far end of the field. Here take path DB24 straight on, climbing over a fence and passing through a hedge gap. Now turn right and follow the right-hand hedge around the bottom of a field past some cottages. Where the hedge turns right, follow it to a hedge gap onto a road at Terrier's End. Turn left onto this road and follow it to a sharp left-hand bend. Here leave the road and take path DB31 right of a telegraph pole straight on into a field, then go straight on over a rise to a stile right of an ash tree into a hedged lane (byway TU36). Turn left into this lane, re-entering Hertfordshire, then turn immediately right into another hedged lane (byway TU34) which leads you over a rise. Where this lane forks, take the right-hand option and follow this for some 350 yards, swinging right and climbing until you enter Stubbing's Wood. At a T-junction just inside the wood, turn left onto byway TU28, then at a fork, keep right, following the wider track to another T-junction. Here turn left onto byway TU75. Just before a gate at the edge of the wood, turn right onto path TU31, soon passing through a squeeze-stile and following the inside edge of the wood straight on for a third of a mile with views to your left over the Tring Bypass and western part of the town. On nearing the bypass, join path TU30 which merges from your right, then at a T-junction, turn right onto a grassy track uphill into a field. Here bear left following the bypass fence over a slight rise, where there are fine views across Tring to Pitstone cement works and Ivinghoe Beacon, to reach a gate and stile. Now take path TU26 straight on beside the bypass fence through two more fields to a concrete track descending to a gate and kissing-gate into Hastoe Lane. Cross this road, then turn left along its footway passing under the A41 and continuing to the edge of Tring. At a T-junction turn right then immediately left into Akeman Street following this past the Tring Zoological Museum to reach the High Street. Here turn right for your starting point.

WALK 11: Marsworth (Startop's End)

Length of Walk: 6.7 miles / 10.8 Km

Starting Point: Entrance to Tring Reservoirs Car Park, Startop's End, Marsworth.

Grid Ref;: SP919141

Maps: OS Landranger Sheet 165
OS Pathfinder Sheet SP81/91
Chiltern Society FP Map No. 18

How to get there / Parking: Startop's End, 6 miles east of Aylesbury, may be reached from the town by taking the A41 towards Tring to Aston Clinton, then turning left onto the B489 and following it for 2.8 miles to Startop's End. Here just before the 'White Lion' and canal bridge traffic lights, turn right into the Tring Reservoirs Car Park.

Marsworth, with its much-altered twelfth-century church on a prominent hillock at the foot of the Chilterns, is perhaps best known today for the Tring Reservoirs immediately to the south of the village. These were constructed between 1802 and 1839 to supply water to the Grand Junction Canal (since 1929 known as the Grand Union Canal) and today, as well as being popular with anglers, they are frequented by many rare species of water birds and have therefore been designated as a nature reserve. Within the parish are also the junctions of the main Grand Union Canal (constructed between 1793 and 1806) and its Wendover and Aylesbury arms. The latter is noted for its interesting double lock a few yards from the canal junction which takes the canal down into the Vale of Aylesbury. In the half century between the construction of these canals and the coming of the nearby London & North Western main railway line, the canals, which were the brainchild of the third Duke of Bridgewater and his engineer friend, James Brindley, provided the major freight link between London and the industrialised Midlands and North.

The walk, which is of an easy nature, is, indeed, one for the lovers of water as much of it follows the towpaths of the three canals and the banks of the reservoirs, including the beautiful tree-line cutting near Bulbourne. Fine views can also be obtained in places of the nearby escarpment and Vale of Aylesbury.

Starting from the entrance to the Tring Reservoirs car park at Startop's End (pronounced 'Starrups'), take path MW12 walking half the length of the car park then turning right up a flight of steps to reach path MW13 on the banks of Startop's End Reservoir. Turn left onto this and where the path forks by a causeway separating the Startop's End and Marsworth Reservoirs, fork left following path MW14 along the top of the bank until it joins the Grand Union Canal towpath (MW16) at Lock No. 40. Now take this towpath straight on for 1.3 miles, after half a mile crossing a bridge over the mouth of the disused Wendover Arm, then passing the canal workshop and 'Grand Junction Arms' at Bulbourne (pronounced 'Booburn') before going under the B488 (Upper Icknield Way) road bridge to enter the beautiful wooded cutting which marks the highest point of the canal. After a further two-thirds of a mile the path climbs a slope to the Marshcroft Lane bridge where you turn right onto this pleasant, little-used road and follow it for half a mile to its end at Tring Grove on the outskirts of Tring.

Turn right here into Grove Road and follow it for over a third of a mile to a filling station on the left. Now after a further two houses, turn left onto path TU66, an alleyway between the houses, and follow it to the B486. Cross this road and take New Road straight on. On nearing a right-hand bend, just past the Air Training Corps hut, turn right through a gate onto path TU78 which is macadamed at first, then becomes unsurfaced. Where the path forks, keep left and follow an obvious path to a gate onto the B488 (Upper Icknield Way). Turn left onto its pavement then having crossed a bridge over a small stream, turn right onto path TU52, a macadam road beside a stream. By some buildings the road ends and you follow a path beside the stream straight on until it joins the Wendover Arm. Now turn left and follow the bank of this disused canal for nearly half a mile to Little Tring where it becomes dry. Here follow a path straight on through an area of scrub then up a flight of steps to Little Tring Road.

Cross the road and a stile and take path TU67 down a flight of steps into a field, then follow the bank of the dry canal until a farm track crosses it. Here turn left across the field to a stile. Having crossed this, turn right onto path TR46 following a right-hand fence uphill to cross a stile at the top, where there is a fine view of Wilstone Reservoir ahead. Now go straight on downhill to a stile into scrubland.

Within the scrubland cross the dry canal, then ignore a stile ahead and turn left onto raised path TR47 and follow this former towpath through scrub. After a quarter mile turn right down a bank and over a stile onto path TR49 which follows a right-hand fence then a belt of scrub downhill. At a corner of the field turn left and follow a right-hand hedge to the next corner. Here go straight on through a hedge gap, then turn right onto a grassy track following a right-hand hedge. Having passed through another hedge gap, bear half left across the next field to cross a stile left of an ash tree in the far corner. Now take path DB6 following a right-hand stream to a footbridge and stile. Cross these and bear half left across the next field heading towards a stile in the far corner. About 50 yards short of this, turn right onto worn path DB5 crossing the field to cross a stile and footbridge in the far corner. Now ignore a gate to your right and take fenced path TR44 through a belt of trees. On emerging over a footbridge onto the bank of Wilstone Reservoir, follow this for nearly half a mile to the next corner of the reservoir. Having just rounded this, turn sharp left onto path TR45 dropping steeply to the B489 (Lower Icknield Way).

Turn left onto this ancient road, then after some 30 yards turn right over a concealed stile onto path TR33. Now bear half right across a paddock to a pair of rail stiles, then bear slightly left across a second paddock to a stile, footbridge and second stile in the far corner. Cross these and a concrete drive, then go straight on through a handgate and across the corner of a field to a handgate leading to a footbridge and kissing-gate onto a road. Turn right onto this road, then almost immediately left through a kissing-gate and take path TR34 bearing half left across a field to a further kissing-gate by a field gate at the end of a village street at Wilstone.

Wilstone, which has only had its own church since 1860, is associated with a story of witchcraft, as in 1751 a suspected witch called Ruth Osborn was hounded by the local populace and murdered by a chimneysweep called Colley who allegedly held her head under water in a local pond. While some say these events took place at nearby Long Marston, what is definitely known is that Colley was hanged for it at Hertford Gaol four months later and his body was brought back and hung in chains at nearby Gubblecote as a warning to local people not to take the law into their own hands.

Follow the village street to Wilstone war memorial, then turn right into Rosebarn Lane. Where its macadam surface narrows and turns left into a housing estate, take path TR29, a grassy lane, straight on to cross a stile, then follow a right-hand hedge straight on to the far end of the field. Here turn left for a few yards, then turn right over a stile and go straight across a field passing left of a telegraph pole to reach a hedge gap leading onto the towpath of the Aylesbury Arm of

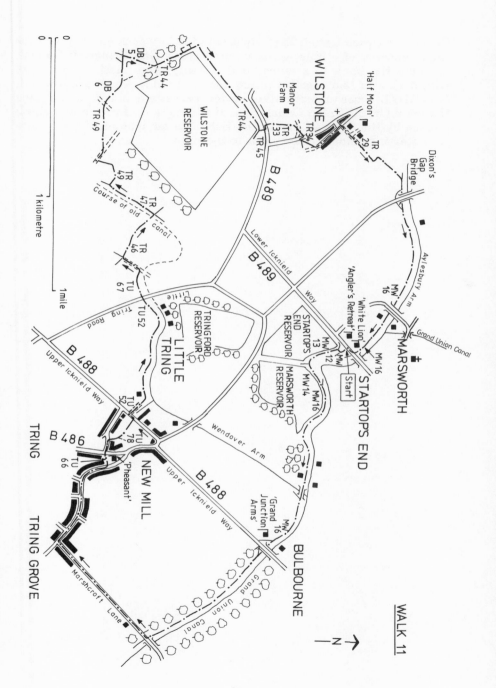

WALK 11

N →

65

the Grand Union Canal. Turn right onto this towpath and follow it for three-quarters of a mile, going under Dixon's Gap Bridge (if flooded, climbing the bank to a stiled road crossing) and passing four locks with a view of Marsworth Church ahead. At Marsworth the towpath (now MW16) goes under another bridge, passes a double lock and joins the main Grand Union Canal, then at Startop's End you finally climb a slope by the 'White Lion' to the B489 (Lower Icknield Way) where your starting point is a few yards to the right.

WALK 12: Pitstone Hill

Length of Walk: (A) 7.4 miles / 11.9 Km
                        (B) 6.5 miles / 10.5 Km

Starting Point: Pitstone Hill car park.

Grid Ref: SP955149

Maps: OS Landranger Sheet 165
         OS Pathfinder Sheet SP81/91
         Chiltern Society FP Map No. 19

How to get there / Parking: Pitstone Hill, 3 miles northeast
of Tring, may be reached from the western end of the town
by taking the B488 towards Dunstable for 3.7 miles. Just
after a narrow railway bridge with traffic lights, ignore a
right-hand turn for Tring Station and Aldbury, then at a
sharp left-hand bend, take a right turn also signposted to
Aldbury. After nearly half a mile, at the top of a rise and
opposite a footpath sign, turn right into an unmarked car
park.

Notes: Heavy nettle growth may be encountered in the
summer months particularly on paths IV1 and AB50.

Pitstone Hill, near the Buckinghamshire/Hertfordshire
boundary, rising to a height of 715 feet, marks the
commencement of the treeless downs of the northern end of
the Chiltern Escarpment which contrast with the wooded
ridges further south. Since the clearance of encroaching scrub
by the Chiltern Society in the late 1970s, regrowth has been
controlled by the traditional method of sheep-grazing. Just
below the hill is the old village of Pitstone, formerly known as
Pightlesthorne, with its fine thirteenth-century church, which
is dwarfed by the neighbouring cement works and its vast
chalk quarries. Beyond is the village of Pitstone Green which
has grown considerably to house the cement workers and is
now joined to Ivinghoe with its magnificent cruciform
thirteenth-century church, fifteenth-century inn, sixteenth-
century town hall and other fine buildings, while in the fields
nearer to the hills stands a restored postmill dating from 1627.

Both walks first take you along the ridge above these
villages, where superb views abound, with Walk A including

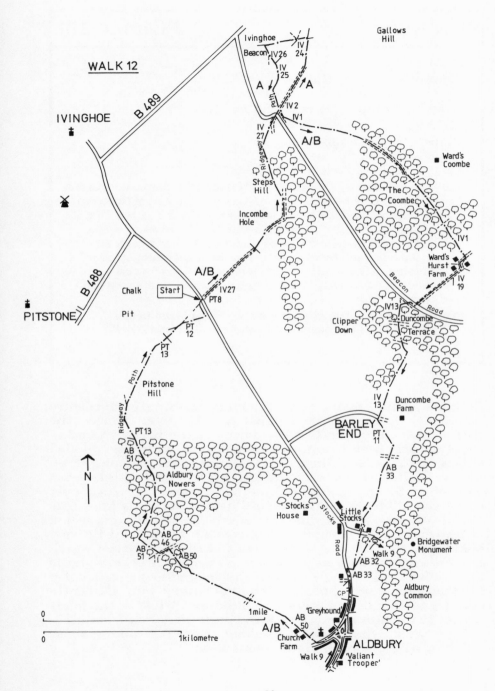

WALK 12

IVINGHOE

B 489

PITSTONE

B 488

Chalk Pit

Start

Ivinghoe Beacon

IV 26

IV 24

IV 25

A

A

IV 2

IV 1

A/B

IV 27

Ridgeway

Steps Hill

Incombe Hole

A/B

IV27

PT8

PT 12

PT 13

Path

Pitstone Hill

Ridgeway

PT13

AB 51

Aldbury Nowers

AB 46

AB 51

AB 50

Gallows Hill

Ward's Coombe

The Coombe

IV 1

Ward's Hurst Farm

IV 19

Beacon

Road

IV13

Duncombe Terrace

Clipper Down

IV 13

Duncombe Farm

BARLEY END

PT 11

AB 33

Stocks House

Little Stocks

Stocks Road

Walk 9

AB 32

AB 33

CP

Bridgewater Monument

Aldbury Common

'Greyhound'

AB 50

Church Farm

A/B

Walk 9

ALDBURY

'Valiant Trooper'

N

0   1mile

0   1kilometre

68

an additional loop to the summit of Ivinghoe Beacon, which at 756 feet provides panoramic views in all directions. Both walks then lead you through woodland to cross a ridge and descend to the picturesque village of Aldbury in its sheltered valley, before returning via Aldbury Nowers and over the crest of Pitstone Hill to your starting point.

Starting from the vehicular entrance to the Pitstone Hill car park, cross the road and take the Ridgeway Path (PT8) opposite, following a grassy track (soon path IV27) straight on for a third of a mile to a gate and stile. Cross the stile and go straight on to the corner of an area of scrub where you join a track. Follow this track skirting a deep, steep-sided coombe called Incombe Hole to your left and climbing steadily to reach a gate and stile near the top of Steps Hill. Do not cross the stile, but bear slightly left passing between the edge of the coombe and the fence to reach open downland. Here go straight on to a marker post at the edge of a belt of scrub, then follow the waymarked path through the scrub. On emerging onto open downland with superb views to your left, follow the right-hand fence straight on downhill to a stile. Cross this and follow an obvious worn path over a rise and down again to a stile leading to a chalky track. Turn left onto this to reach a bend in Beacon Road, then step over a chain opposite.

Here **Walk B** turns right onto path IV1 following a grassy track towards a gate, then turning right onto a chalky path to a squeeze stile. Now read the next paragraph. **Walk A** takes a chalky track (path IV2) straight on to cross a stile by a gate. Now bear half left along a grassy track across a field to a gate and rails, then bear slightly left following a worn path steeply uphill to the crest of the ridge where wide views open out with Edlesborough with its prominent fourteenth-century church backed by Totternhoe Knolls ahead and the Dunstable Downs to your right. Here turn left onto path IV24 following the crest of the ridge uphill to a stile. Cross this, ignore a crossing path and go straight on uphill to the Beacon with its panoramic views. Now turn left onto path IV26 taking the left-hand of two worn paths downhill, soon joining path IV25. After a third of a mile you cross your outward route and follow a chalky path straight on to a squeeze stile.

Here **Walks A and B** do not go through the squeeze stile, but turn left over a conventional stile on path IV1 and follow a left-hand fence for a quarter mile. Where the fence turns left by an old gate, leave it and go straight on, passing right of a clump of hawthorn bushes, to reach a gate and stile into a wood called The Coombe. In the wood, follow a wide grassy track straight on for a quarter mile, then, where it ends, bear left, soon entering a cypress plantation. Go straight on through this plantation, then, having passed the corner of a left-hand field, follow a high wire-mesh fence straight on uphill to a rail stile into the corner of a field. Cross this stile and follow the outside edge of the wood, then a right-hand fence, straight on uphill to a gate near Ward's Hurst Farm. Turn right through the gate onto path IV19, taking an obvious track straight on between farm buildings into a farmyard. Here bear left, then right onto a concrete farm road and follow this for a quarter mile to reach Beacon Road.

Turn right onto this road, then, after about 50 yards, turn left onto path IV13 into a wood called Duncombe Terrace. Just inside the wood, turn right onto a well-used path, then, after about 20 yards, fork left onto a branching path. At a T-junction by a twin-trunked tree, turn left onto a wider track and follow it downhill to reach a major crossing track. Here take an ill-defined path straight on downhill. In the bottom of the dip, ignore a crossing path and go straight on uphill to a stile into a field corner. Cross this and follow the outside edge of the wood straight on, disregarding a stile into it, then, by a corner of the wood, cross a stile and continue to follow its outside edge downhill with fine views towards Aldbury ahead. Where the edge of the wood begins to bear away to the right, leave it, bearing slightly left across the field and passing just left of two telegraph poles to reach the end of a road at Barley End by the gate to Duncombe Farm.

Cross this road and a rail stile opposite onto path PT11, bearing half left across a field to a concealed stile in the next hedge. Having crossed this, go straight across the next field towards a gate at the Hertfordshire boundary. Here ignore a crossing track and cross some rails beside the gate, then take path AB33 following a right-hand fence to cross a stile by a gate. Now follow a left-hand fence through two fields to a gate and stile, then take a macadam drive straight on past a house to a road. Here go straight on over a stile and across a field to cross a stile under the tallest tree in the next hedge (where you join the reverse direction of Walk 9). Now turn right and follow the right-hand hedge to a corner of the field where you cross a stile and descend steps onto Stocks Road – BEWARE BLIND BEND – LISTEN FOR TRAFFIC! Turn left onto this road and follow it into the picturesque village of Aldbury.

On reaching the village centre, where the road forks, keep right (leaving Walk 9) passing the 'Greyhound', the village pond and seventeenth-century timbered manor house and the village green with its ancient wooden stocks which were in use till the 1830s. At a T-junction, turn right into Station Road leaving the green and passing the fourteenth-century church where the novelist, Mrs Humphry Ward, niece of Matthew Arnold and aunt of Aldous and Julian Huxley, who lived at Stocks House, was buried in 1920. Just past the church, turn right over a stile by a gate onto path AB50 and go straight across a field to a gate. Go through this, then bear slightly left to cross a stile by the corner of a modern barn at Church Farm. Now follow a path between the barn and a hedge until you emerge into a farm storage area. Here follow the hedge to a stile, then go straight on along a fenced path to a stile into a fenced bridleway. Cross the bridleway and a stile opposite, then bear slightly left to the corner of a hedge on the slope of the next rise. Here cross a stile and follow a right-hand hedge uphill to reach the corner of a wood. Go through a hedge gap into the wood and follow an obvious winding path until you reach a sunken way (path AB46). Turn left onto this and after about 40 yards, turn right onto path AB51 (the Ridgeway Path). Now follow its obvious waymarked course for two-thirds of a mile through a mixture of woodland and scrubland on Aldbury Nowers with fine views to your left across the Tring Gap in places, until a stile at the county boundary leads you out onto the open downland of Pitstone Hill. Here take path PT13, continuing to follow an ancient earthwork which you have been following for some distance, to the top of Pitstone Hill. Near the corner of a fence, leave the earthwork and follow the fence straight on along the ridge for over half a mile, ignoring the stile of a crossing path and later joining path PT12, to reach a stile into the end of the car park.

WALK 13: Aldbury Common

Length of Walk: 7.1 miles / 11.4 Km

Starting Point: Bridgewater Monument turning off B4506 at Aldbury Common.

Grid Ref: SP979128

Maps: OS Landranger Sheets 165 & 166
OS Pathfinder Sheets SP81/91 & TL01/11
Chiltern Society FP Map No. 19

How to get there / Parking: The starting point, 3 miles north of Berkhamsted, may be reached from the town by taking the old A41 (A4251) to Northchurch, then turning right onto the B4506 and following it for 2.7 miles. About two-thirds of a mile past the Aldbury turn, turn left onto the macadam road to the Bridgewater Monument and park as soon as possible.

Notes: Heavy nettle growth may be encountered in summer particularly on parts of bridleway LG10 and path LG12.

Aldbury Common is one of a belt of several mostly wooded commons extending from the outskirts of Berkhamsted to Aldbury village and across the Bucks boundary to the Chiltern escarpment. When the Ashridge Estate was sold in 1929, a large area of these commons was acquired by the National Trust which has done much to facilitate public access. Ashridge House, which can be seen at the eastern end of Prince's Riding (where the car park is located), was commissioned by the third Duke of Bridgewater before his death in 1803 to replace a mediaeval house which had formerly been a monastery. Designed in the neo-Gothic style by James Wyatt and his nephew, Sir Jeffry Wyatville, the house was completed in about 1820 and since 1959 has been a management college. At the other end of the Riding, which forms part of the landscaping carried out by Capability Brown and amended by Repton, is the Bridgewater Monument erected in 1832 in memory of the third Duke of Bridgewater who is noted as 'the Father of the English canal system'.

The walk first explores parts of the wooded Aldbury and Berkhamsted Commons before crossing Golden Valley to the south-eastern end of Little Gaddesden. From here it takes you across a small valley to Hudnall Common, another National Trust property, then downhill to the Beds boundary in the Gade valley, before returning via the north-western end of Little Gaddesden and Ashridge Golf Course to your starting point.

Starting from the entrance to the road to the Bridgewater Monument, take the B4506 southwards for a few yards, then turn right onto bridleway AB21, a grassy path into the woods. Follow it straight on for a third of a mile, ignoring three crossing paths. On reaching path AB12, a wide crossing track with a National Trust sign 'Footpath only – No horses', turn left onto it. At a five-way track junction go straight on, at one point passing a field to your left. Just before a left-hand pond, turn left onto a crossing track (bridleway AB14). After about 100 yards at a fork take the waymarked right-hand lesser alternative (path AB15) and follow it straight on, passing left of some large beech trees, to reach the B4506.

Cross this road and turn right onto its walkable verge to reach a road junction. Here turn left onto bridleway NC33, a rough track into a large clearing. Go straight on along the right-hand edge of the clearing. At its far side take a grassy path straight on through the trees. Ignore a branching path to the right and on reaching a wide crossing track, turn left onto it. After a few yards at a crossways turn right onto a wide grassy track (still NC33) and follow it straight on for a third of a mile. Just past Little Coldharbour Farm, join a stony track and follow it straight on to a track junction by Coldharbour Farm. Here bear slightly right, crossing a track leading to the farm and taking a rough bridle track straight on into the woods. At a three-way fork at the bottom of a slope, take the left-hand option (bridleway NC48) bearing half left and follow this track out to the edge of an arable field. Here bear half left again and follow the outside edge of the woods for nearly half a mile to a corner of the field then go straight on through woodland to reach the Ashridge road.

Cross this road and take path LG7, a macadam drive opposite. Follow this uphill, ignoring a right-hand fork, until you reach a house called Rodinghead. Here leave the drive and take a fenced track straight on between fields to cross a stile by a gate. Now go straight on downhill across a large field heading for and passing through a clump of trees. Here keep straight on downhill into Golden Valley crossing a stile at one point and heading for a tall beech tree at the edge of Cromer Wood left of a fenced pumping station compound. Go straight on into the wood, climbing the steep slope diagonally until you reach an old iron gatepost at the corner of a wall. Now take a sunken path uphill beside the wall through laurel bushes to reach Nettleden Road at Little Gaddesden.

Cross this road and turn right onto its pavement. Just past Shepherd's Cottage, turn left through white gates onto bridleway LG10 into Home Farm. By the farmhouse gates bear slightly left off the concrete drive into a narrow bridleway leading between a fence and a wall to a bridlegate. Now turn right then immediately left round the end of a stable block, then go straight on through the left-hand of two gates leaving the farm and taking a fenced track downhill with a view of Little Gaddesden House to your left. In the valley bottom do **not** go through the gate ahead, but turn left and follow the fenced bridleway to the corner of the right-hand field. Here turn right and climb a hill to enter a copse at the edge of Hudnall Common.

Just inside the copse, ignore two lesser branching paths to the left and follow the bridleway straight on through the copse and some scrub to reach a road. Now take bridleway LG10 straight on across open common, with views across the Gade valley towards Studham ahead, heading for single oak then continuing straight on to reach a well worn track into scrubland. Take this track straight on downhill through the scrub ignoring two crossing paths. After a quarter mile, at a fork bear left to join Hudnall Lane near the Bedfordshire boundary.

Cross this road and take chalky path LG15 opposite, turning left alongside the road and gradually bearing away from it through scrubland. At a fork keep left, soon emerging onto open common. Bear half right across the common to the far right-hand corner, then take a waymarked path straight on through a narrow strip of woodland to an access road to houses along the edge of the common. Bear slightly right onto this road (path LG14) and at a right-hand bend by the entrance to Meadow Farm, fork left onto a path signposted to Little Gaddesden. Take this path straight on between hedges to a kissing-gate into a field, then follow the right-hand hedge straight on to cross a stile (where you meet the route of Walk 17). Here take path LG12 bearing half left across a large field, passing left of an oak tree to reach a stile about 80 yards right of the far corner. Now go straight on to cross a stile just right of the corner of the next field, then continue straight on to cross a stile onto Church Road, which leads to Little Gaddesden's fifteenth-century church (described in Walk 17). Bear slightly left across this road and another stile, then bear half left across a paddock, passing the rear corner of a garden to reach a kissing-gate near the far corner of the paddock. Go through this and follow a narrow fenced path round the backs of gardens to another kissing-gate leading into a field. Now cross this field diagonally to a kissing-gate in front of a red-roofed house at Little Gaddesden.

Go through this and turn right onto a road then immediately left

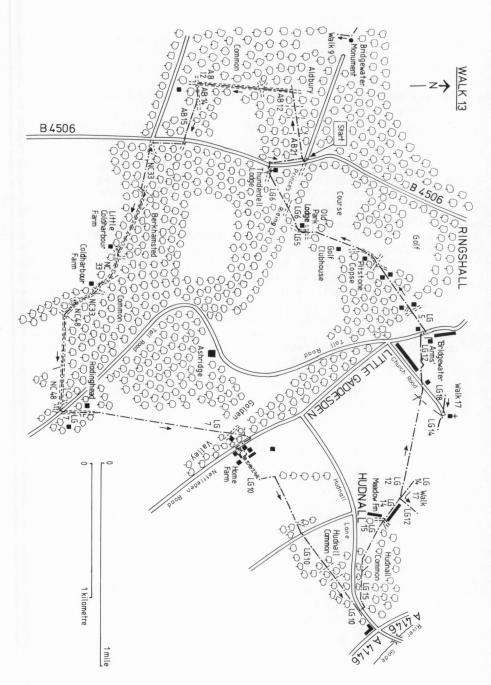

WALK 13

N→

75

onto path LG5 through the 'Bridgewater Arms' car park to a stile in its rear fence. Now follow a fenced path downhill to a macadam access road. Cross this and bear slightly left into a hedged path, soon crossing a further drive and continuing straight on until you enter a wood. Here go straight on uphill, soon crossing a golf tee and a track, then keep straight on through woodland and between garden fences to reach a macadam drive. Turn left onto this, then at a T-junction turn right, then immediately left onto a macadam drive (still LG5). Go straight on past a bungalow called Pitstone Copse, then at the far end of its garden leave the drive and keep straight on, following the edge of a left-hand copse across the golf course, then continuing straight on between the clubhouse and several greens to a worn track leading into woodland ahead. On reaching a track junction by Old Park Lodge, bear slightly left passing left of the house. By the far end of its garden bear half right onto path LG6 leaving the track and crossing the golf course diagonally, passing right of a green and aiming for a single birch tree at the edge of the fairway. Pass right of this tree then go straight on through a belt of trees to reach Prince's Riding, which gives you a brief glimpse to your left of Ashridge House. Cross this ride and take a woodland path straight on, passing through a clearing near a building and soon emerging onto a macadam drive. Turn right onto this and follow it to a gateway by Thunderdell Lodge onto the B4506. Cross this and turn right onto a rough path along its verge back to your starting point.

Length of Walk: (A) 8.8 miles / 14.2 Km
                         (B) 6.2 miles / 10.0 Km
                         (C) 5.0 miles / 8.0 Km

Starting Point: (A/B) Unmarked car park in Dodds Lane,
                                    Piccott's End.
                         (C) Corner Farm road junction,
                                    Gaddesden Row.

Grid Ref;   (A/B) TL052095
                   (C) TL066117

Maps: OS Landranger Sheet 166
          OS Pathfinder Sheets TL00/10 (A/B only) & TL01/11 (all)
          Chiltern Society FP Map No. 20 (all Walk B / part of
          Walks A/C only)

How to get there / Parking: (A/B) Piccott's End, on the
    northern edge of Hemel Hempstead, may be reached from
the town centre by taking the A4146 towards Leighton
Buzzard to a roundabout at its junction with the A4147.
Here turn right onto the A4147, then at the next
roundabout turn left into Piccott's End. Go straight on
through the village for half a mile. Where the right-hand
houses end, turn right into Dodds Lane and follow it for
some 300 yards, then turn left through a hedge gap into a
small unmarked car park.
    (C) Corner Farm, Gaddesden Row, 3 miles north of Hemel
Hempstead, may be reached from the town by taking the
A4146 towards Leighton Buzzard to the 'Red Lion' at
Water End. Here turn right onto the road signposted to
Flamstead and Markyate and follow it for 1.8 miles to a
T-junction at Gaddesden Row. Now turn right and follow
the road for 0.8 miles to a road junction by Corner Farm,
where you can park on the wide grass verges.

Notes: Heavy nettle growth may be encountered in places in
summer on all three walks, while bridleway GG42 on Walks
A & C may be very muddy in places even in dry weather.

Piccott's End, on the River Gade, only a mile north of the
centre of Hemel Hempstead, is still an attractive village in a
relatively unspoilt setting despite the fact that the town's

WALK 14

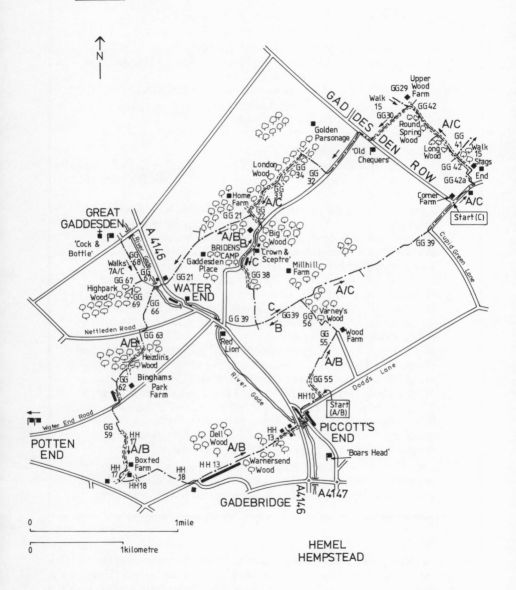

rapidly expanding housing estates have covered the tops of the hills on either side of the valley. In 1953 mediaeval wall-paintings were discovered in a fifteenth-century cottage in the village called Hall House, which also has a priest hide and a mediaeval well.

All three alternative walks pass close to Gaddesden Place on the slopes of the Gade valley above Water End. This house was originally built for the Halsey family in 1768–1773 by James Wyatt, who later designed Ashridge, but had to be largely rebuilt after a disastrous fire in 1905. In addition, Walks A and C explore the peaceful plateau to the east of the Gade valley, while Walks A and B cross and recross the scenic Gade valley visiting the picturesque hamlet of Water End and exploring the hills to the west

Walks A and B start from the unmarked car park in Dodds Lane, Piccott's End, and take path GG55 leading out of the car park up a rough hedged lane, the right-hand hedge of which soon peters out. Where the track turns right across the field, continue along it to the corner of a hedge. Now go through a hedge gap and follow a winding right-hand hedge straight on uphill to cross a stile with views behind of Hemel Hempstead and the Gade valley. Here follow the right-hand hedge straight on, then, where it turns right, go straight on across the field to a stile by a tree in front of the farmhouse at Wood Farm. Do not cross this stile, but turn left onto path GG56 crossing the field to an oak tree. Here go straight on, joining the edge of Varney's Wood and following it, at one point turning left, to double-gates and a stile at a corner of the wood. Cross this stile and continue along the edge of the wood. Where this turns right, follow a field boundary straight on to reach crossing bridleway GG39 by the end of a belt of trees. For **Walk A** now omit the next paragraph.

Walk B turns left here onto bridleway GG39 and follows its winding course downhill beside a left-hand hedge for a quarter mile to the bottom corner of the field. Now turn right through a hedge gap onto path GG38 and follow a right-hand hedge uphill, eventually with a young plantation to your left. Just before reaching a mature copse ahead, turn left onto a track across the plantation to a hedge gap where there is a fine view behind you towards Hemel Hempstead. Go through this gap and take a grassy track uphill to some garages. Here turn left onto a stony track which leads you to a road at Briden's Camp. Turn right onto this winding road and follow it for a third of a mile, passing the 'Crown & Sceptre' and rounding first a sharp left-hand, then a sharp right-hand bend. Some 130 yards beyond the right-hand bend, turn left onto path GG22, the concrete road towards

Home Farm. Where its concrete ends, turn left over a stile by double-gates onto path GG21 rejoining **Walk A**. Now omit the next four paragraphs.

Walk A turns right onto bridleway GG39, joining **Walk C**, then **Walks A and C** follow the outside edge of the tree-belt. At the far end of the tree-belt, continue through a hedge gap and follow a left-hand hedge straight on through three fields for nearly a mile with views of the modern outskirts of Hemel Hempstead to your right. Near the far end of the third field, descend into a sunken gully to join Cupid Green Lane at a sharp bend. Now follow this narrow road straight on downhill and up again for a quarter mile to reach the Corner Farm road junction at Gaddesden Row.

At the Corner Farm road junction (**the start of Walk C**), **Walks A and C** take the Redbourn road straight on. After about 330 yards, opposite double-gates, turn left onto fenced bridleway GG42, then turn immediately left over a stile onto fenced path GG42a. Follow this path beside the bridleway, turning right then left. On reaching another stile, cross it, the bridleway and a further stile opposite. Now continue between fences, turning left by a house and passing a paddock to reach a stile back onto bridleway GG42 at the edge of a wood. Take the bridleway straight on to the far side of the wood, then by a red metal gate to your right, take a green lane straight on (joining the reverse direction of Walk 15), soon passing Long Wood and a field to your left and entering Round Spring Wood. Take the bridleway through the wood soon transferring through a gap in the right-hand hedge to the other side of the hedge and continuing between it and a fence to Upper Wood Farm.

Here (leaving Walk 15 again) turn left onto a farm road (path GG30) and follow it for a third of a mile to the Gaddesden Row road near the 'Old Chequers'. Turn right onto this road, then at a junction, turn left onto the Water End and Hemel Hempstead road and follow it for a third of a mile. Just past the bottom of a dip, turn right through a hedge gap onto path GG32 following a right-hand hedge to the far side of the field. Here go straight on into the middle of a crossing avenue of lime trees, then turn left onto path GG34, a grassy track along the avenue. Where the track bears left and leaves the avenue, follow it, immediately forking right onto path GG33 along the outside edge of the avenue, then the edge of London Wood. On reaching the flint road to Home Farm (path GG22), turn left onto it. Just before it becomes concreted, **Walk A** turns right over a stile by double-gates onto path GG21, then omit the next paragraph.

Walk C takes path GG22 straight on along the concrete road, then turns right onto a public road and follows it for a third of a mile. Having passed the 'Crown and Sceptre', at a sharp right-hand bend, turn left onto path GG38, a stony track beside some farm cottages with a fine view down the Gade valley to Hemel Hempstead. On reaching some garages, turn right onto a grassy track and follow it past a copse to a hedge gap. Go through this gap, then bear half left along a track across a young plantation to reach a hedge in a dip. Here turn right and follow the near side of the hedge downhill to a hedge gap in the bottom corner of the field. Go through this gap, then turn left onto well-worn bridleway GG39 and follow its winding course uphill for a quarter mile to rejoin **Walk A** by a belt of trees. Now go back four paragraphs.

Walks A and B now take path GG21 bearing slightly right across parkland with a view to your right of Home Farm, a good example of a technologically advanced Victorian farm, to cross a stile just right of some large oaks where the imposing façade of Gaddesden Place comes into view ahead. Now bear slightly right across a parkland field to another stile in the far corner of the field. Having crossed this, turn left, following the left-hand fence through an outcrop of trees, then bear slightly right across a field to a gate and handgate. Go through the handgate and bear half left to a stile, then keep straight on to a further stile left of a large hollybush where there are fine views of Great Gaddesden and the Gade valley and of Gaddesden Place behind you. Now bear slightly left downhill passing between a conifer and an oak to a stile, then cross the corner of another field to a further stile with a fine view of Water End with its picturesque seventeenth-century brick and timber cottages ahead. Here bear slightly left, aiming for an ash tree just left of a white cottage to reach the corner of a garden fence. Follow the fence straight on past the cottage towards the road to a stile onto the garden path and a handgate leading onto the A4146 at Water End.

Cross this road and turn right, then turn immediately left onto path GG66 leading between garden walls to two stiles. Having crossed these, bear half right, following a fence at first to reach a footbridge over the River Gade. At the far end of this bridge, turn left (still on GG66) and follow the river to a footbridge over a small watercourse, then go straight on, gradually deviating from the river to reach a stile. Cross this and bear slightly right to join a right-hand fence then follow it, ignoring a stile in it, to reach a stile onto Nettleden Road. Turn right onto this road, then after about 60 yards, turn left over a stile onto path GG63. Now go straight on uphill, passing left of a single beech tree, to reach a track into Heizdin's Wood. Before entering the wood, turn round for a fine view across the valley then follow the track uphill through the wood ignoring a crossing path. On leaving the wood, bear half right across a field to the left-hand of two small oak trees, then bear slightly left to reach a storm-damaged beech tree at the end of a hedge. Here bear half left onto path GG62 along the far side of the hedge to a stile by an old gate. Cross this and go straight on, soon joining a gravel drive and following it to Water End Road on the edge of Potten End.

Turn right onto this road and at a right-hand bend, turn left through a small gate onto fenced path GG59. On crossing a stile, follow the sporadic right-hand hedge straight on, then after about 50 yards, by an oak tree, go through a gap in the hedge and walk downhill between it and a wire fence to a fence gap at the bottom. Go through this and turn left (now on path HH17), then turn right over a stile by a New Zealand (barbed-wire) gate onto a fenced farm track uphill to Boxted Farm. Where the track ends, go straight on through a fence gap by a New Zealand gate and continue ahead until you reach a wooden fence. Now turn right and follow this fence, turning right and later left through a hedge gap to a stile onto the farm drive. Turn right onto this, then immediately left over a stile onto path HH18 and bear half left, following a left-hand fence to cross a stile onto a fenced track. Now bear half right to cross a further stile by a gate, then follow a right-hand fence straight on to a stile at the far end of the field. Turn right over this and follow the left-hand hedge through two fields to a road on the edge of Hemel Hempstead.

Turn left onto this road, then at a right-hand bend, leave it and take path HH13 straight on through a hedge gap. Now follow the edge of a field straight on beside gardens. At its far end, cross a stile and continue between a hedge and a fence. Where the fence ends, follow the outside edge of Warnersend Wood, then a right-hand hedge straight on. At the far end of the field, bear slightly right to pass through a squeeze-stile, then continue along a fenced path. On reaching a bend in a track, join it and follow it straight on past a wood and farm buildings to reach a macadam drive, then continue along this through gates soon reaching the A4146. Cross this road and go straight on across a bridge over the Gade to reach the village street in Piccott's End. Turn left onto this and after some 130 yards, turn right into Dodds Lane. About 30 yards up the lane, where a left-hand hedge begins, leave the road and take path HH10 following the back of the roadside hedge to a hedge gap into the car park.

```
┌─────────────────────────────────────────────────────────────┐
│  WALK 15:                            Redbourn                │
├─────────────────────────────────────────────────────────────┤
```

Length of Walk: 9.1 miles / 14.6 Km

Starting Point: Car park near cricket pitch on Redbourn Common.

Grid Ref: TL103119

Maps: OS Landranger Sheet 166
OS Pathfinder Sheet TL01/11

How to get there / Parking: Redbourn, 4 miles northeast of Hemel Hempstead, may be reached from the town by taking the B487. After passing under the M1, turn left onto a road signposted to Church End and follow it straight on for half a mile to a car park to your left on Redbourn Common.

Notes: Heavy nettle growth may be encountered in the summer months, particularly on path FS45, while bridleway GG42 may be very muddy in places even in dry weather.

```
└─────────────────────────────────────────────────────────────┘
```

Redbourn in the Ver valley, the name of which means 'reedy stream' suggesting that the area was once marshy, is set around an extensive and very attractive common where cricket has been played since 1666. At the southwestern end of the common is the original village known as Church End where a street of picturesque cottages leads to the twelfth-century church, noted for its carved oak rood screen dating from 1478. East of the common is the village High Street on the line of a Roman road called Watling Street. This road, which has now been bypassed by the A5183 (formerly A5), was particularly busy in the eighteenth and early nineteenth centuries when it formed the main stagecoach road from London to Birmingham, Liverpool and Holyhead and thus inns and other buildings sprang up here during this period to service the coaches. Before the construction of the M1, the age of the motor-car brought another flood of heavy traffic to the High Street, but with the bypass it is now relatively peaceful again. Finally, north of the common is an area of modern housing estates which have swelled the population to 6,000, but nevertheless this is only a small development in

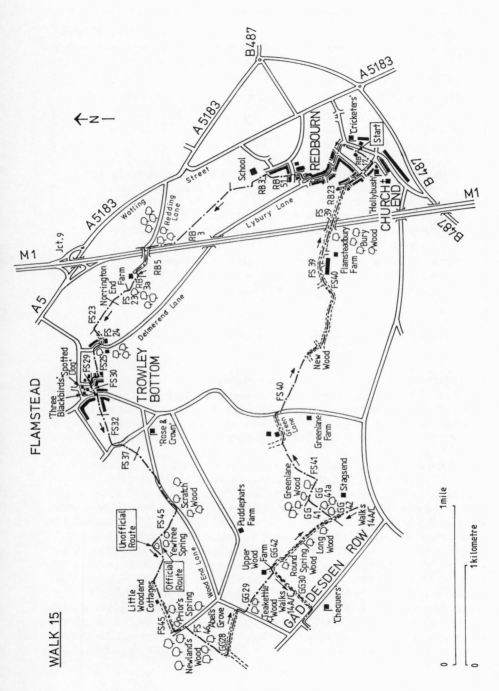

WALK 15

84

comparison with what would have occurred if the one-time plan to make Redbourn the site of a new town had been implemented.

The walk takes you out of Redbourn over the hills to the west of the Ver valley to the hilltop village of Flamstead. From here, it takes you southwestwards through remote hill country to near the scattered community of Gaddesden Row before returning through equally remote hill country to Redbourn.

Starting from the back of the car park on Redbourn Common, turn right onto macadam path RB17 within a fine avenue of lime trees (briefly interrupted on one side by the cricket pitch) and follow it to Lybury Lane. Turn left onto this road and follow it straight on for over a third of a mile, crossing the common and passing through a housing estate. On reaching an open green in the middle of the estate, turn right onto a road round the edge of the green, then take the first road leaving the green to reach a T-junction. Here turn left into Snatchup, then at a second T-junction, cross a road called Long Cutt and take hedged path RB51 straight on to a gate into a recreation ground. Enter the recreation ground, then bear slightly right across it to the far end of a wire-mesh fence. Here turn right following a right-hand fence to a hedge gap into enclosed macadam path RB3. Turn left onto this path and follow it straight on for 200 yards, ignoring branching paths to your left until a fence forces you to turn left into a field. Now follow a right-hand hedge, almost immediately turning right. Where the hedge ends, follow the right-hand fence straight on, then, where the fence turns right, go straight on along a grassy path, later passing through a gap in the vestiges of a hedge and following the right-hand side of a line of trees. On reaching a more solid hedge, keep left of this and follow it straight on to the boundary fence of the M1. Here bear half right, following the M1 fence through a wood and a field to a gate and stile onto Redding Lane, where you obtain a fine view of the Ver valley.

Turn left onto this road, crossing a bridge over the M1, then just before reaching Norrington End Farm, turn left over a stile by a gate onto path RB5 and go straight across a field to the corner of a hedge by a large elm stump. Here take path RB3a crossing a stile and following a sporadic right-hand hedge past the farm with a fine view of the Ver valley ahead. Where the hedge swings right, bear half left across the field to concealed stiles in the left-hand hedge. Cross these and turn right onto path FS23, following the right-hand hedge downhill. Where this hedge turns right, go straight on downhill across two fields to a stile at the far side of the second field. Now bear slightly left uphill to a stile under a crab-tree to the right of the top left-hand corner of the field. Do **not** cross this stile, but instead turn left onto path FS24 and follow the right-hand hedge to the corner of the field. Here enter a hedged lane and follow it straight on to Delmerend Lane. Turn right onto this road, then, after about 100 yards, turn left onto path FS25, another hedged lane. On emerging in a field, follow the right-hand hedge straight on to a kissing-gate into a fenced alleyway leading to a residential road in Flamstead.

Flamstead, a corruption of 'Verlamstead', is an attractive village set on a hilltop above the Ver valley. The village, when seen from afar, is dominated by its magnificent twelfth-century church with its massive tower containing Roman bricks and its interior boasting some fine mediaeval murals and later marble monuments.

Turn right onto this road and follow it round left- and right-hand bends, then turn left through a kissing-gate into the churchyard. Here, if wishing to visit one of the village pubs or look at the attractive village centre, take the right-hand path (FS29) passing right of the church. Otherwise, take path FS30, the left-hand of the three paths through the churchyard, to a gate and gap leading to Trowley Hill Road. Turn left onto this road, then immediately right onto path FS32, a fenced alleyway leading you out past a housing estate into a field. Now go straight on across the field, passing a telegraph pole and then heading for a hedge gap left of an ash tree in tall bushes ahead. Go through this gap and turn left onto a narrow road called Pietley Hill. At a left-hand bend, turn right over a stile onto path FS37 and go straight on downhill to cross a stile at the bottom.Now bear slightly right uphill to a gap in a hedge ahead leading into Wood End Lane where there is a fine view behind you across the valley to Flamstead.

Turn right onto this road then just after Scratch Wood begins to your left, turn right over a stile by a gate and follow path FS45 beside a left-hand fence, then along the outside edge of a wood called Yewtree Spring. Here it is currently necessary to take an unofficial diversion, as the official route through the wood is blocked by fences. If a stile is provided into the wood, turn left over it; otherwise continue to a hedge gap at the far end of the field, where there is a fine view of Flamstead behind you. Now turn left, still following the outside edge of the wood to its far end where you rejoin the official path. Here bear half right across the field, with views ahead across these remote hills towards the distant Bedfordshire village of Studham, to a stile in a hedge just right of a corner of the field. Cross this and turn left, following a left-hand hedge and fence and ignoring a stile step in a horse-jump to your left. On nearing Little Woodend Cottages, where the left-hand fence diverges from the hedge, cross a stile in the fence and keep left of a shed to join a drive by the cottages. Take this drive straight on to reach a road then turn left onto it and follow it through Newlands

Wood. Just after a slight left-hand bend turn right over a stile onto path FS46 and bear slightly left across a field passing the corner of a copse called Abel's Grove to cross a stile by an old gate in the far corner of the field. Here turn left into a green lane and follow it to a right-hand bend, then turn left through a hedge gap onto path GG28 following a grassy track beside a right-hand hedge for over a quarter mile to a road. Turn right onto this road then after about 80 yards turn left through a hedge gap onto bridleway GG29 following a fenced track beside a right-hand hedge to Upper Wood Farm.

Here, on reaching a farm road (path GG30), if wanting refreshments turn right onto it to reach the 'Old Chequers', Gaddesden Row, in just over a third of a mile. Otherwise, join the reverse direction of Walk 14, crossing the farm road and taking bridleway GG42, a fenced track left of a five-bar gate, straight on beside a right-hand hedge. On reaching the corner of Round Spring Wood, follow the track into and through the wood to reach a field. Here follow the fenced bridleway straight on beside a left-hand hedge to enter Long Wood, then continue through it and along a hedged lane until you reach the beginning of a third wood, left of the lane. Leaving Walk 14, turn left here through a red metal gate onto path GG41, following the outside edge of the wood straight on. Where the edge of the wood turns right, go straight on downhill to reach the edge of Greenlane Wood, then turn right onto path GG41a following it. At the far end of the wood, turn left through a hedge gap onto path FS41 following the outside edge of the wood, then a left-hand hedge uphill. Where the hedge turns left, bear slightly right across the field, heading for an ash tree in the hedge ahead, to reach a hedge gap into Green Lane. Bear slightly right into this appropriately-named lane and follow it passing a cottage to reach a T-junction with a macadam road.

Here turn right and follow the road for some 60 yards. Just past a telegraph pole turn left onto path FS40 following a crop-break, later a hedge, for some 700 yards to reach New Wood. Now join a track and follow it straight on for over half a mile, ignoring all branching tracks and eventually reaching a macadam farm road near Flamsteadbury Farm. Turn right onto this road (bridleway FS39, later RB23) and follow it past the farm and over the M1 into Redbourn. On reaching the village, take this road called Flamsteadbury Lane straight on to Redbourn Common. Here take West Common straight on then just before Church End to your right, turn left onto macadam path RB17 within the avenue of lime trees and follow it back to your starting point.

WALK 16: Markyate

Length of Walk: 4.9 miles / 7.9 Km
Starting Point: 'Sun Inn', Markyate.
Grid Ref: TL062164
Maps: OS Landranger Sheet 166
OS Pathfinder Sheet TL01/11
How to get there / Parking: Markyate, 3.5 miles southwest of Luton, may be reached by leaving the M1 at Junction 9 (Flamstead). Now take the A5 towards Dunstable and fork left onto the road into the village. On reaching the village centre, find a suitable on-street parking place in one of the side-streets.

Markyate, formerly known variously as Markyate Street or even Market Street, grew up as a long straggle of mainly eighteenth-century buildings along Watling Street, the Roman road from Dover via London, Verulamium (St. Albans) and Durocobrivae (Dunstable) to the West Midlands, and has only in recent years spread out substantially from this road. Although the village was bypassed by the modern A5 in 1957, a number of old coaching inns still bear witness to the fact that the main road used to run through the village. To the north of Markyate is its Georgian parish church built in 1724 in a park known as Markyate Cell because it was in mediaeval times the site of a nunnery. The present house with this name, built in 1825, replaced an earlier one which, in the seventeenth century, had been the home of a widow named Lady Katherine Ferrers. Legend has it that she became a highwayman and later haunted both the old house and the A5. Earlier in the same century, the village also featured in national events when the servant of Ambrose Rookwood, one of the conspirators in the Gunpowder Plot, was arrested at the 'Sun Inn' in 1605. Some 130 years later, Markyate was also the location of a boarding school attended by the young William Cowper of Berkhamsted who was later to achieve fame as a poet.

The walk, which includes some fine views, first takes you out of Markyate and the Ver valley and explores the hill country on the Bedfordshire boundary to the north of the

village before recrossing the Ver valley near Kensworth Lynch and following the top of its southern slope to Markyate.

Starting from the 'Sun Inn' in Markyate High Street, follow the High Street southeastwards for about 60 yards, then turn left into Hicks Road and follow it out to the A5. Cross the main road by way of a footbridge and at the far end of it, turn left down a flight of steps and cross the extension of Hicks Road. Now take a macadam road opposite, called The Ridings, straight on to a gate and stile at the end of the road. Cross the stile and take path MY7, bearing slightly right across a field to cross a stile at the left-hand end of a hedge. Now bear half left across the next field to the near corner of a garden hedge. Keep left of this hedge and follow it straight on, then, where the hedge turns right, continue straight on to join a drive which leads you out to the B4540.

Cross this road, turn right onto its pavement and follow it for a third of a mile, ignoring a side-turning and passing a row of bungalows. Opposite a water-tower in the trees to your right, turn left over a stile onto path MY8 and bear half right across a field, heading between two electricity poles ahead to reach a stile. Cross this and bear half right heading for the distant Caddington Church to cross a stile at the county boundary at the far side of the field. Here turn left onto an unnumbered path crossing another stile and following a left-hand fence to a stile at the far side of the field. Cross this and follow a fenced path, ignoring a gap in the left-hand fence and entering a right-hand field. Now take path CA22 following the left-hand hedge straight on to a gate into Pipers Lane on the edge of the Bedfordshire village of Aley Green.

Turn right onto this road and follow it through Aley Green to a T-junction by Piper's Farm. Here turn left and after some 130 yards, turn left again over a footbridge and through a hedge gap onto path CA19, following a right-hand hedge uphill at first then on the level. On reaching a corner of the field, turn right onto path CA18, keeping left of a sporadic hedge and following it through two fields with views of Caddington to your right ahead. At the far end of the second field, do **not** go through the hedge gap, but instead turn left onto path CA17 and follow a right-hand hedge for a third of a mile to gates into Millfield Lane. Turn right onto this road, then just past a white house, turn left through a hedge gap onto path CA17/MY10, following a left-hand hedge to reach a copse. Go straight on through the copse, then continue across a field past an oak tree to a gap in the next hedge. Drop down though this gap and go straight on downhill with views across both spurs of the Ver valley ahead to cross a stile just left of an ash tree. Now continue straight on downhill to a gate and stile in the bottom left-hand corner of the field leading to the A5.

Here cross the A5 bearing slightly left to a hedge gap opposite the entrance to a nursery, then take signposted path KN12 through this gap and straight on uphill across a field to reach the end of a hedge at the hilltop. Now turn left and follow the near side of the hedge downhill to a footbridge over a ditch, which is all there is of the River Ver near its source at Kensworth Lynch.

Cross this bridge and turn right onto the B4540. After a few yards turn left through double gates onto path KN13, a farm track which climbs steadily to reach a Dutch barn, where there are fine views of the Ver valley to your left. Where the track turns right by the Dutch barn, follow the left-hand hedge straight on. About 100 yards short of the far end of the field, turn left through a hedge gap onto path KN2 and bear half right across the corner of a field to reach another hedge gap. Go through this gap and take path MY13 following a grassy track straight on beside a left-hand hedge, with views ahead of Flamstead on a distant hilltop and through gaps in the hedge of the Ver valley including Markyate Cell in its wooded park. At the far end of the field, cross a stile by a gate and follow a left-hand fence straight on beneath a power line past Manor Farm to a kissing-gate at the far end of the field. Go through this gate and follow the left-hand hedge past a cricket field, the village hall and a children's playground into an alleyway leading to Cavendish Road in Markyate. Turn left onto this road, following it downhill to the High Street, then turn right to reach your starting point.

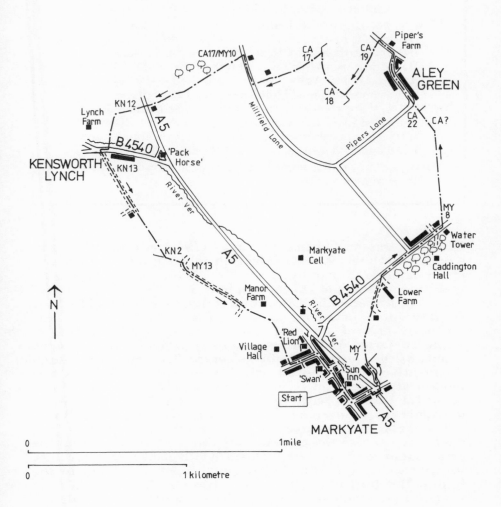

CADDINGTON

WALK 16

Piper's Farm

ALEY GREEN

CA 17/MY 10

CA 17

CA 19

CA 18

CA 22

CA?

Lynch Farm

KN 12

A5

Millfield Lane

Pipers Lane

KENSWORTH LYNCH

B4540

'Pack Horse'

KN 13

River Ver

MY 8

Water Tower

KN 2

A5

Markyate Cell

B4540

Caddington Hall

MY 13

Lower Farm

N

Manor Farm

River Ver

'Red Lion'

MY 7

Village Hall

'Swan'

Sun Inn

Start

A5

MARKYATE

0   1 mile

0   1 kilometre

91

WALK 17:   Studham

Length of Walk: 6.4 miles / 10.3 Km
Starting Point: Crossroads by 'Red Lion', Studham.
Grid Ref: **TL023158**
Maps: OS Landranger Sheets 165 & 166
            OS Pathfinder Sheets SP81/91 & TL01/11
            Chiltern Society FP Maps Nos. 19 & 20

How to get there / Parking: Studham, 4 miles south of
    Dunstable, may be reached from the town by taking the
    B489 towards Aston Clinton, then forking left onto the
    B4541 towards Whipsnade and the Downs and following
    it for 2.2 miles. At its junction with the B4540, take the
    Studham and Hemel Hempstead road straight on for 1.6
    miles, then, at a crossroads in the village by the village
    hall, 'Red Lion' and war memorial clocktower, there is a
    small car park on the left. If full, turn right into Church
    Road and find a suitable on-street parking place.

Notes: Heavy nettle growth may be encountered in places in
    the summer months.

Studham, the southernmost village in Bedfordshire, nestles in
a hollow in the backland of the Dunstable Downs, surrounded
by an extensive upland plateau. Until 1897, the village, which
was once a centre of the straw-plait industry and was one of
the early strongholds of Nonconformity, in fact, straddled the
Hertfordshire boundary and it was only then that the
southern half of its extensive common and many of its
scattered farms and cottages were transferred to the same
county as the church and village centre. The cement-rendered
thirteenth-century church, which is somewhat isolated and
hidden at the end of its cul-de-sac lane, has a surprisingly
beautiful interior with fine carved stone capitals and an
unusual carved Norman font pre-dating the present building.

The walk, which traverses three counties, leads you first
westwards across the plateau past the church to descend the
escarpment to the Buckinghamshire village of Dagnall, before
turning south and climbing through quiet woodland to the
hilltop Hertfordshire village of Little Gaddesden. You then
return northeastwards to Studham, on the way skirting

**Hudnall and crossing the upper reaches of the Gade Valley.
Although basically an open walk with fine viewpoints, some
pleasant woodland provides variety.**

Starting from the crossroads by the 'Red Lion' at Studham, take
Church Road, then turn right onto path ST18 striking off between
Studham Methodist Church and a road called Swannell's Wood. Now
cross a stile in a hedge gap and follow a left-hand hedge through two
fields, joining Walk 18 in the second field. At the far end of this field,
take path ST19 following a grassy track which bears half right to the
corner of a hedge and tree belt concealing Studham churchyard then
bears half left and follows the churchyard hedge to a crossing track.
Here take path ST21 straight on over a stile, following a right-hand
fence past two oak trees, then bear slightly left diverging gradually
from the fence to reach a stile and footbridge into a wood called
Church Grove.

Inside the wood, disregard a crossing bridleway (onto which
Walk 18 turns right) and follow a well-defined track straight on until
you reach a signposted T-junction. Here turn onto path ST23 and
follow this track to a crossing track at the edge of the wood. Now go
straight on, leaving the wood by a gap to the right of the horse-jump
ahead. Follow the edge of the wood, later a left-hand hedge, straight
on to a hedge gap at the far end of the field. Go through this and bear
slightly right across the next field to a concealed hedge gap just
beyond a slight kink in the right-hand hedge. Go through this gap
onto Buckinghamshire path ED15, then bear slightly right across a
golf course, keeping right of a green and fairway ahead to reach a
marker post by a large tree stump. Here bear slightly left following
the left-hand edge of a tree belt. At the far end of this tree belt, bear
slightly left passing left of a tee to reach the right-hand end of a short
section of hedge, then go straight on across a tee to a rail stile into
woodland. Here follow a fenced path straight on downhill, ignoring a
crossing drive and continuing for some 350 yards to a rail stile. Cross
this and follow a right-hand fence beside a drive to a handgate leading
into Studham Lane. Turn right onto this road, then, shortly after a
left-hand bend, turn left over a stile onto path ED15, following a
left-hand fence straight on across two fields and a car park to the
A4146 at Dagnall.

Turn right onto this road, passing the 'Golden Rule'. Just past
Cross Keys Farm on the left, turn left over a stile by a gate onto path
ED18, passing the end of a wooden fence and bearing slightly left to a
hedge gap leading to a farmyard. Here go straight on past some farm
buildings. Near the back of the farm, by a building with a wooden
tower numbered '6' and '7', turn left onto a track between the

buildings. Follow it, bearing slightly right out of the farm and through a hedge gap, then beside a left-hand hedge. Where the track turns right, leave it and bear slightly right across the field to its far corner. Here bear slightly left onto Hertfordshire bridleway LG1, crossing the next field to the corner of a hedge. Now bear left of the hedge and follow it to a farm track. Turn right onto this (soon on bridleway ED12), heading towards Well Farm until you reach a left-hand hedge gap. Turn left through this, keeping left of a fence and swinging right beside a right-hand hedge (soon on LG1 again). Where the hedge ends, go straight on across a field to a bridlegate. Go through this gate, then bear slightly left across a field to a wicket-gate into Hoo Wood.

Inside the wood, follow the obvious bridleway straight on uphill, ignoring all crossing tracks until, after more than a third of a mile, you reach a bridlegate into a field. Here follow the right-hand hedge straight on across the field to a gate and bridlegate. Go through the bridlegate and follow a left-hand fence straight on to a stile in it. Turn left over this onto path LG18 and bear half right across a field to the corner of a fence by a tall oak tree. Follow this right-hand fence straight on to a kissing-gate, from which the fifteenth-century church of Little Gaddesden comes into view ahead.

This church is principally notable for the wealth of memorials which it contains to members of the Egerton family, the Earls and Dukes of Bridgewater, who held nearby Ashridge Park from 1604 to 1849, including one to the third and last Duke who inspired the construction of the Grand Union Canal and is consequently known as 'The Father of British Inland Navigation'.

Now go straight on across a field to a kissing-gate leading to Church Road, then follow this straight on past the church to a stile opposite the second gate into the churchyard. Turn right over this, then immediately left onto path LG14, following a left-hand fence at first. Where this fence bears away to the left, leave it and go straight on across the field to a concealed stile in the hedge ahead. Cross this and follow a left-hand hedge straight on for a third of a mile to a stile near an oak tree, where you meet but do not join the route of Walk 13. Do **not** cross this stile, but instead turn left through a hedge gap onto path LG12 and follow a right-hand hedge downhill through two fields (later on bridleway LG11, then ST33) to reach the A4146 in the Gade valley above the source of its river.

Cross this main road, go through a gate opposite and take bridleway ST25 following a left-hand hedge uphill through two fields. On nearing the top corner of the second field, go through a bridlegate in the left-hand fence and follow a right-hand hedge uphill to a gate into Ravensdell Wood. Go through this and follow a track through the wood to another gate, then follow a right-hand hedge for a few yards

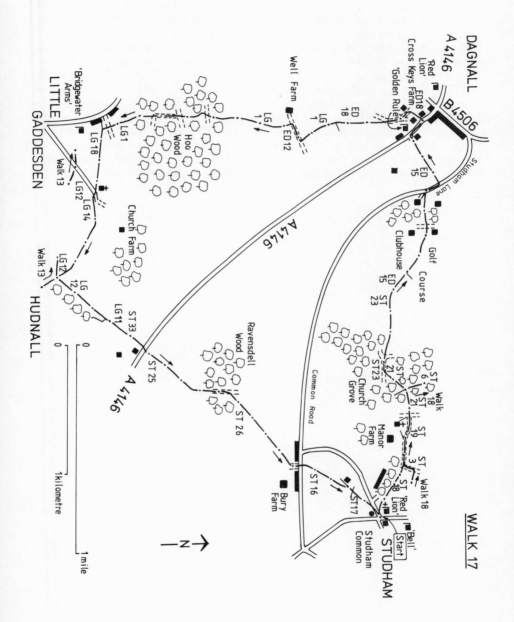

WALK 17

to a stile in it. Turn right over this onto path ST26, then bear half left across a large field, heading towards some distant houses on the edge of Studham to reach a stile. Cross this and bear slightly right across the next field to a stile and gate left of a large red-brick house leading into a lane. Follow this lane out to Common Road and cross this, bearing half right to a hedge gap. Go through this and take path ST16, bearing half right across a field following what is normally a crop break to the right-hand corner of a large house ahead which was formerly the village school. Here bear right through a gap onto Studham Common, following bridleway ST17 along the valley bottom, then through a belt of scrub. On emerging onto open common by a football pitch, bear left to meet Church Road opposite the Methodist Church, then turn right onto this road for your starting point.

WALK 18: Whipsnade Downs

Length of Walk: (A) 6.8 miles / 10.9 Km
(B) 2.5 miles / 4.0 Km

Starting Point: Whipsnade Downs National Trust car park.

Grid Ref: TL000184

Maps: OS Landranger Sheet 166
OS Pathfinder Sheet TL01/11

How to get there / Parking: Whipsnade Downs, 2.5 miles southwest of Dunstable, may be reached from the town by taking the B489 towards Aston Clinton for 2.5 miles to the 'Plough Inn' roundabout. Here turn left onto the B4506 towards Dagnall, then, after a quarter mile, turn left again onto the B4540 up Whipsnade Downs. Near the top, look out for the signposted Whipsnade Downs Car Park on your left.

Notes: Deep mud may be encountered on bridleway WP1 even in dry weather, as may heavy nettle growth in the summer months.

Whipsnade Downs and nearby Dunstable Downs both provide a rural playground for nearby built-up areas, the lofty location of which offers panoramic views over the Ouzel valley and beyond, as well as a pleasant breeze even on the hottest day. The nearby village of Whipsnade, which is visited by both walks, is notable for the extensive green around which its scattered cottages are situated and being the highest village in Bedfordshire. Its brick-built church has a sixteenth-century tower and eighteenth-century nave but incorporates some details of an earlier building, while at the back of the village is the Tree Cathedral planted in the 1930s by E.K.Blyth in memory of friends killed in the First World War and now looked after by the National Trust. However what Whipsnade is best known for is the Wild Animal Park which was opened by the Royal Zoological Society in 1931 to exhibit its hardier animals in natural surroundings. The Wild Animal Park in its scenically spectacular setting can be toured by a steam railway which you may hear in the course of your walk.

Both walks commence by taking you along the crest of the Downs with superb views before making for Whipsnade

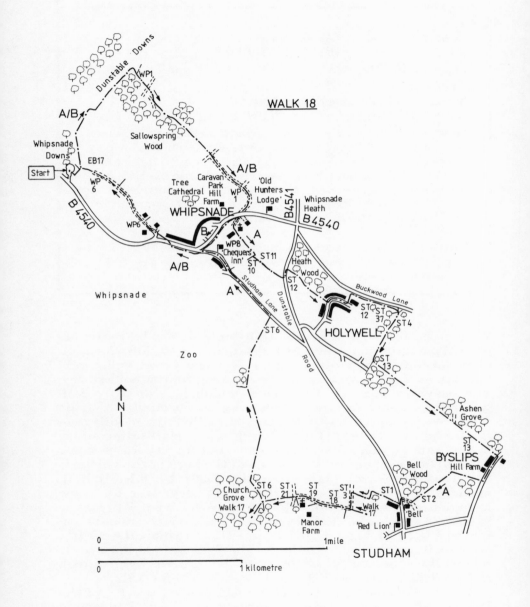

WALK 18

village, while **Walk A** additionally explores the upland plateau around Studham with its pleasant mixture of woods and farmland.

Starting from Whipsnade Downs Car Park, **both walks** climb a flight of steps on its east side, then turn left onto a National Trust permissive path, ignoring a crossing bridleway and soon emerging through a gate onto open downland. Now follow a right-hand hedge later a fence straight on, wiggling to your right at one point, with panoramic views to your left including Ivinghoe Beacon, the prominent fourteenth-century Edlesborough Church on its hillock, Totternhoe Knolls, the site of a Bronze Age fort and Norman castle and later Dunstable Downs ahead. After half a mile, at the far end of Sallowspring Wood to your right, turn right following the fence of the wood to a bridlegate in the field corner. Go through this and take fenced bridleway WP1 straight on along the edge of the wood, soon crossing a macadam drive and continuing beside the wood, now with a hedge to your left. On approaching a track in woodland to your right, do **not** join it but bear slightly left into a sunken way, still following the edge of the wood, then passing through it to reach a gate. Now take the fenced bridleway straight on along the edge of a field to a crossing track, then take a green lane straight on downhill, eventually ignoring a branching lane to your left and shortly emerging onto Whipsnade Green. Here follow a grassy track bearing right uphill to reach the B4540.

Having crossed the road, **Walk B** turns right and follows the B4540 verge to a sharp right-hand bend. Here cross a side-road and now read the last paragraph. For **Walk A** ignore a macadam drive to your left and take a grassy track straight on across the green to the churchyard gate. Take path WP8 into the churchyard, leaving the gravel path and passing right of the church then bearing half left to cross a concealed stile in the back hedge. Follow a left-hand hedge to cross a stile by a gate, then turn right onto path ST10 over another stile by a gate. Now turn left onto path ST11 following a left-hand hedge to the far side of the field. Here go through a hedge gap and turn left into Dunstable Road. On reaching a corner of Heath Wood to your right, turn right through a hedge gap onto path ST12 and follow the outside edge of the wood to the far side of the field. Here take a fenced path straight on between gardens to a road called Woodland Rise at Holywell.

Turn left onto its pavement and follow it round a bend. Just past house no. 25 turn left onto a fenced path (still ST12). Shortly before the far end of the left-hand fence, fork right onto a woodland path, soon passing the backs of a number of gardens and becoming ST37. After a quarter mile at a crossways take path ST4 straight on, soon bearing right and following the inside edge of the wood uphill. On emerging into a field, follow a right-hand hedge straight on then at the far side of the field take a fenced path straight on along the outside edge of a wood. After some 70 yards turn left into the wood onto ill-defined path ST13 which takes you straight across the wood ignoring two crossing paths. At the far side of the wood, go straight on across a field to the near right-hand corner of a copse called Ashen Grove. Follow its outside edge straight on to the far end of the copse, then go straight on across the field, passing right of a tree to reach the corner of a hedge. Now follow this hedge straight on to the back corner of a garden, then take a fenced path straight on beside the garden to a road at Byslips.

Turn right onto this road and follow it for over 200 yards passing Hill Farm. At a double bend turn right over a stile onto path ST2 and go straight across a field to cross a stile then bear slightly left, passing the corner of a copse and continuing to a gate and stile at the far side of the field. Cross the stile and follow a right-hand hedge downhill and up again to cross some rails by a gate at the corner of Bell Wood. Now go straight on through two paddocks and Studham allotments to reach a track. Bear right onto it and follow it to Dunstable Road by the 'Bell'. Turn left onto this road then immediately right onto path ST1, keeping right of a concrete wall and following it, soon with a hedge to your right. Where the wall ends, take the fenced path straight on, soon passing through a copse. On entering a field, turn left and follow a left-hand hedge around two sides of the field, then turn left onto path ST3, a grassy track following a right-hand hedge. At the far side of the next field ignore a stile ahead and turn right onto path ST18 (joining Walk 17), then follow this grassy track beside a left-hand hedge. At the far side of the field take the track straight on through a hedge gap, then bearing half right (now on path ST19) to the corner of a tree-belt surrounding Studham churchyard. Here follow the track bearing half left past the churchyard to reach a crossing stony track, then take path ST21 straight on over a stile, following a right-hand fence past two oaks and then bearing slightly left and diverging from the fence to reach a stile and footbridge into a wood called Church Grove.

Cross these and (leaving Walk 17) turn right onto bridleway ST6 along the inside edge of the wood. Where this forks, go right, leaving the wood and taking a grassy track beside a right-hand hedge straight on through two fields to enter a copse. Here ignore a branching bridleway to the left and go straight on through the copse, then continue between the perimeter fence of Whipsnade Wild Animal Park and a thick hedge for a third of a mile to Studham Lane. Turn left onto this road and follow it straight on for nearly half a mile, ignoring a left-hand fork and emerging by the 'Chequers' onto Whipsnade Green.

Just before the junction of Studham Lane and the B4540, fork left onto a worn path along the verge of the B4540 rejoining **Walk B**. **Walks A and B** now follow the B4540 verge to the beginning of a triangular green on the other side of the road. Here cross the road and take a worn path across the rear of the green to join a macadam access road. Follow this straight on to its end, then go straight on through double gates onto fenced bridleway WP6. After passing a bungalow, continue straight on, now climbing gently between hedges for a third of a mile to the top of Whipsnade Downs, where the bridleway (now EB17) begins to descend again and reaches open downland. Here bear half left to reach the steps leading down into the car park.

WALK 19: Dunstable Downs

Length of Walk: 6.8 miles / 10.9 Km

Starting Point: Entrance to the main car park on Dunstable Downs.

Grid Ref: TL008198

Maps: OS Landranger Sheets 165 & 166
OS Pathfinder Sheets SP82/92, TL01/11 & TL02/12

How to get there / Parking: Dunstable Downs car park, 1.5 miles south of the town centre, may be reached from it by taking the B489 towards Aston Clinton, then turning left onto the B4541 towards The Downs and Whipsnade. At the top of the hill, park in one of the right-hand car parks near a low building with a pointed roof (the visitor centre and toilet block).

Notes: Deep mud may be encountered on TT12, even in dry weather, while heavy nettle growth may also be found in summer, particularly on path TT23.

The Dunstable Downs, with their spectacular views along the Chilterns to Ivinghoe Beacon and out across the Vale of Aylesbury towards Oxfordshire and the Cotswolds, are today a real 'honeypot' for people from Dunstable, Luton and farther afield, for picnics and walks with superb views and convenient parking. Four thousand years ago, these hills must also have been frequented, as at the northern end of the Downs are the Five Knolls, five huge Neolithic or Bronze Age burial barrows, where excavations have not only revealed remains from this period, but also a large number of skeletons originating from the fifth century AD, some of whom had injured bones or their hands tied behind their backs suggesting that they were the victims of some battle or massacre.

Much of the walk, indeed, traverses terrain which has yielded evidence of early settlement, as, after passing the Five Knolls, you descend to the junction of the Ancient British Icknield Way and the equally ancient Green Lane, before following Green Lane past the Bronze Age camp known as Maiden Bower and modern lime pits and continuing to Totternhoe with its Bronze Age hill fort, Norman castle earthworks and mediaeval stone pits at Lower End and the site of a Roman villa at Church End. In addition to its historical aspects, the walk also provides a series of fine views and visits places of flora and fauna interest and so has something to offer for everyone.

Starting from the entrance to the main macadamed car park on Dunstable Downs by the visitor centre and toilets, bear half right across the car park to a macadam path out of its rear right-hand corner. Where this path bears right towards the visitor centre, leave it and take a mown grass path parallel to the B4541 straight on along the top of the ridge with fine views to your left towards Totternhoe Knolls and beyond. You soon pass through an overflow car park, then continue straight on to a kissing-gate where you join a worn chalky path. Take this worn path straight on rounding a steep-sided combe called Pascomb Pit, where views across Dunstable open out to your right, and climbing to the summit at the end of the Downs with its superb panoramic views. Now take path D23 straight on, descending gently past the Five Knolls to reach several gates. Here go through a kissing-gate and follow a worn path straight on downhill to a mown green on the edge of Dunstable. Go straight on across the green heading for the left-hand side of a roundabout at the junction of the B489 and B4541.

At the roundabout, cross the B489 (Tring Road), then bear half right, passing through a gap beside a padlocked gate into the appropriately named Green Lane (D4). Now follow this tree-lined lane straight on for three-quarters of a mile, at first between housing estates, then (as TT12) leaving the town behind and ignoring a branching green lane to your left. On reaching a crossing green lane, take TT12, now considerably narrowed by encroaching scrub, straight on for almost another half mile, passing within 150 yards of Maiden Bower hidden by the right-hand hedge. Where the lane widens out and turns left, leave it and take hedged path TT43 straight on, soon with the left-hand hedge giving way to a fence and views opening out across a restored lime pit to your left and towards Stanbridge ahead. After some 350 yards you leave the quarry behind and go straight on downhill through scrubland. Where the path eventually forks, go left (still on TT43), climbing a chalky slope to a stile, then turn left following a left-hand fence with views to your right towards Tilsworth and Stanbridge in places. On leaving the scrub behind, take a grassy track straight on towards Totternhoe Limeworks, soon entering a sunken way and reaching a gate and stile into a green lane. Turn left into this lane (TT2) and follow it for some 250 yards. On nearing the limeworks, ignore a crossing track, then turn right into another green lane (TT42). After about 200 yards, at a junction of tracks, turn left onto bridleway TT24, a rough lane leading to the end of a macadam road at Totternhoe Lower End.

Take this road straight on to the limeworks gates. Here turn left onto fenced path TT23 to the right of the gates and drive, soon turning right, then left, then right again across fields to reach a squeeze-stile leading in a few yards to a green lane (TT1). Turn sharp left onto this, following it up Castle Hill. Some 50 yards before a sharp right-hand bend, turn right over a stile onto path TT28 leading into an undulating area called 'Little Hills' where Totternhoe stone, used amongst other things in the building of Windsor Castle, was excavated from the twelfth century onwards. To your left is the castle mound capped by the earthworks of a wooden Norman castle superimposed on a Bronze Age fort, while its use for defensive purposes by the Saxons is also indicated by the Saxon name of Totternhoe, which means 'look-out house hill'.

Here ignore a branching path to your right and bear slightly left across the undulating ground to a stile near the bottom of the castle mound where there are fine views out across the Ouzel valley into the Vale of Aylesbury, then bear slightly right for a stile into scrubland. Cross this and pass through the scrub into a beechwood, then bear left, ignoring a branching path to your right and following the contours of the hill until you reach a crossing path with steps (TT29). Turn right onto this, descending steeply and eventually reaching a road at Totternhoe Middle End.

Cross this road and turn left along its pavement, passing the thatched, timber-framed 'Cross Keys'. At a left-hand bend, turn right onto path TT21 beside house no. 181, descending between fences into a small field. Now follow its left-hand fence straight on to a footbridge. Cross this and bear half left following a left-hand hedge to cross a stile. Now turn left over a stile by a gate onto path TT19 following a left-hand hedge and stream through two fields. At the far side of the second field, cross a culvert in a hedge gap and bear half right across the next field to the near end of a row of taller trees. Here cross a footbridge and go straight on across a field to a footbridge left of gates ahead, then follow a right-hand hedge straight on. Soon after the hedge ends, turn right over a stile onto path TT20, then bear left across a field, heading for a building with a small turret and weather vane and crossing a sheep-wire fence at one point, to reach a derelict kissing gate. Go through this, then turn left into a lane at Church End and follow it to a T-junction near Totternhoe's fifteenth-century church built in the local stone.

Here turn right into Church Road passing the church. Just after the pavement ends, by a macadam drive, cross the road and a stile opposite onto path TT9, bearing half right across a field to a stile. In

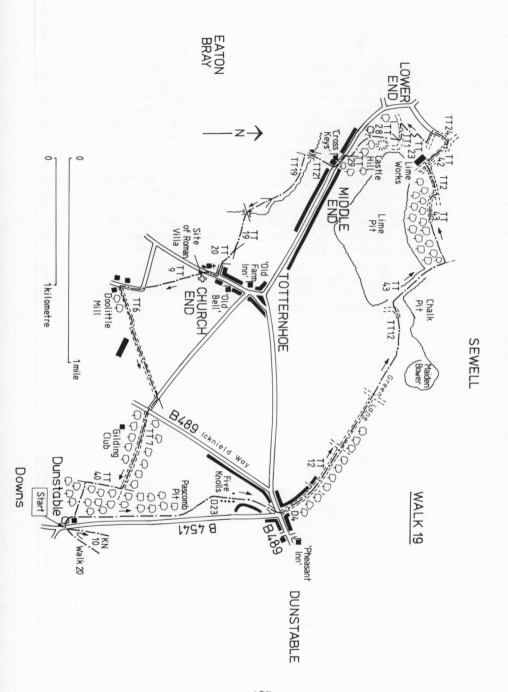

this field, the site of a fourth-century Roman courtyard villa is to your left and there are fine views of the Dunstable Downs ahead. Now go straight on across the next field to a stile and footbridge midway between two clumps of trees, then bear slightly right across a further field to a stile at the corner of a fenceline leading to a bend in a road. Take this road straight on looking out for the remains of a disused wind- and watermill called Doolittle Mill partially hidden by trees ahead. At a right-hand bend just before the mill, turn left onto bridleway TT6, following a track beside a right-hand belt of trees for over half a mile to reach Wellhead Road.

Turn right onto this and at a road junction, cross the B489 and take bridleway TT7, a green lane, straight on towards the Downs. At the foot of the Downs go through two bridlegates, then turn right onto path TT40 following a right-hand fence over a rise into the next dip. Here, just before reaching a bridlegate and kissing-gate ahead, turn left onto a permissive path following a right-hand fence steeply uphill. Half-way up the hill, stop for a rest and turn round for a view across the gliding club airstrip towards Totternhoe, then continue uphill to gates leading to the open hilltop with the visitor centre and toilets and your starting point straight ahead.

WALK 20: Dunstable

Length of Walk: 7.8 miles / 12.6 Km

Starting Point: Salvation Army chapel at junction of Icknield Street, Bullpond Lane and Burr Street, Dunstable.

Grid Ref: TL017216

Maps: OS Landranger Sheet 166
OS Pathfinder Sheets TL01/11 & TL02/12

How to get there / Parking: From the junction of the A5, A505 and B489 in the centre of Dunstable take the B489 (West Street) towards Aston Clinton, then take the second turning left (Icknield Street) where a free car park is on your left.

Notes: Paths D19 and D21 may be affected by the construction of the A5 (Dunstable Bypass) which is due for completion in 1994.

Dunstable, at the crossroads of the prehistoric Icknield Way and Watling Street, a Roman road from Dover via London to Holyhead, is believed to have been inhabited since the Stone Age as archaeologists have made finds dating from various ages in close proximity to the town. Although a Roman staging post known as Durocobrivae was recorded, it is believed not to have been very large and it was only in 1131, when King Henry I founded an Augustinian priory and constructed a royal lodge known as Kingsbury, that 'Dunestaple' (as it was then known) became a place of any size. Originally the Priory was of vast proportions being 320 feet long and having transepts 150 feet wide, but the west towers collapsed in a storm in 1222 and the transepts, central tower, long choir and monastic buildings were at some stage demolished to leave the present parish church with its massive Norman columns, round arches and fifteenth-century north tower. In 1533 the Priory was also the scene of a major historical event as it was here that Thomas Cranmer, the then Archbishop of Canterbury, pronounced the annulment of the marriage of Henry VIII and Catherine of Aragon which led to the English Reformation. In the eighteenth century improved road communications caused Dunstable to become an important

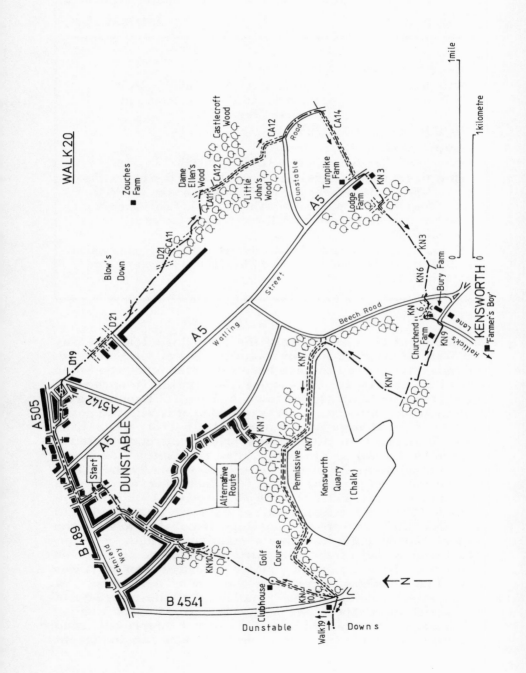

WALK 20

108

port of call for stagecoaches and so the town's inns flourished, as did the local straw-hat industry, but it has only been in the last century that the town has mushroomed into the large industrial town it is today.

The walk, which explores the downland around Dunstable, for which the town is famous, first passes through the town centre before skirting the lofty ridge of Blow's Down, which, to some extent, still separates Dunstable from its larger neighbour Luton. It then leads you across the A5 in its valley to Kensworth Church End in a quiet Chiltern hollow before following a high ridge round Kensworth Quarry to reach the top of the Dunstable Downs. From here your return route traverses a downland golf course with superb views across the town before descending to your starting point.

Starting by the Salvation Army chapel at the junction of Icknield Street, Bullpond Lane and Burr Street, take Icknield Street to the B489 (West Street) (part of the Icknield Way), then turn right and follow it to its junction with the A5 (High Street) (part of Watling Street) and the A505. Here take the A505 (Church Street) straight on past the Book Castle, the parish church and the 'Old Palace Lodge' and 'Norman King' on the site of the royal lodge of Kingsbury. At the far end of the churchyard turn right into Priory Road, then left into St. Peters Road. Disregard one turning to the right and at a second junction, fork right into Bigthan Road then fork immediately left into a fenced alleyway which leads you to a road junction.

Here cross the major road (A5142) bearing slightly right and taking path D19 virtually opposite. Where this path forks, take the right-hand option straight on towards Blow's Down soon passing under a pylon where you ignore a crossing track. On reaching the end of a residential road called Half Moon Lane, take path D21 straight on through a small gate, then keep right of the power lines. At the far end of a row of houses to your right, fork left onto a lesser path soon joining a grassy sunken track. Just before the far end of a line of bushes to your right, fork right to join another sunken way which keeps right of the power lines, then at a fork bear right again to pass right of the next pylon. Now the sunken way begins to climb passing under the power lines, with wide views across the town opening out to your right. Ignore a major crossing track and keep straight on, soon joining a left-hand fence then dropping again to cross a stile. Here take path CA11 straight on through scrub. After some 200 yards ignore a crossing path and go straight on through a hedge into a field. Now turn right and follow a right-hand hedge. After about 150 yards by a marker post, bear half left across the field to a corner of Dame

Ellen's Wood, then follow its outside edge straight on to meet a farm road. Turn right onto this (soon on path CA12) and follow its winding course for half a mile to reach Dunstable Road.

Turn left onto its left-hand pavement and follow it round a long right-hand bend. Where the pavement ends, cross the road and continue along its verge to a left-hand bend. Here turn right over a stile onto path CA14 following a left-hand hedge to the far end of the field, then a right-hand hedge straight on downhill to a stile onto the A5 opposite Lodge Farm.

Cross this road and turn left along it. After some 50 yards turn right just before a large white metal gate onto path KN3 passing a builder's yard to enter a field. Here follow the right-hand hedge straight on uphill to a small gate into a belt of trees then turn right onto a track in the tree belt. After about 60 yards, on reaching a crossing track, turn left, *not* joining the track but passing through a hedge gap left of it. Now follow a right-hand hedge uphill and down again. At the bottom of the dip go through a gap in the right-hand hedge and follow the other side of the hedge straight on uphill. At the top of the rise where the hedge turns left, bear right onto path KN6 crossing the field heading just right of Kensworth Church to reach a grassy track leading to Beech Road.

Cross this road and at the entrance to the drive to Bury Farm, climb its left-hand bank and go through a gap in the holly bushes. Now follow a right-hand hedge parallel to the drive rejoining it where the hedge peters out. On reaching the farm, at a three-way fork bear right following a left-hand hedge and line of trees bordering the churchyard. Where the track turns right across the field, turn left over a stile into the churchyard passing right of the church, which dates from around 1120, to reach its gates. Go through these then bear slightly right through the trees to a road junction.

Here take Hollick's Lane straight on uphill. After about 60 yards turn right through a concealed hedge gap onto path KN9 following a right-hand hedge nearly to the far end of the field. Here about 20 yards beyond a telegraph pole turn right through a hedge gap and follow a left-hand hedge which soon turns left and becomes sporadic. On reaching the edge of a plantation ahead, turn right and follow it soon turning left again. At a corner of the field turn right onto path KN7 following a left-hand hedge gently uphill with fine views opening out to your right down the Ver valley and over the hilltops into Hertfordshire. At the far end of the field go straight on through a hedge gap, then wiggle to your right and follow a left-hand hedge downhill and up again to reach a track near the corner of the Kensworth Quarry fence.

Turn left onto this track and follow it beside the fence of this enormous chalk quarry for nearly half a mile, soon with superb views to your right across Dunstable to Blow's Down and several ranges of hills beyond. Having passed through a kissing-gate, continue to follow the quarry fence to a signposted junction. Here take a signposted permissive path following the quarry fence straight on for a further half mile, now with woodland to your right, until the track leads you out into a field. (NB Should this permissive path be closed for any reason, an albeit less attractive alternative route using public rights of way is indicated on the plan). Now keep to the track bearing right and following the edge of a plantation at first, then entering it. Here ignore a branching path to the right and take a green lane straight on, at one point bearing left, then later passing through a squeeze-stile by a gate and eventually reaching the B4541 opposite the Dunstable Downs car park (the starting point of Walk 19).

If wishing to admire the panoramic views available from the Downs or use the public conveniences, cross the road; otherwise do *not* join it, but turn sharp right onto fenced path KN10 which leads you through a belt of scrub onto a golf course. Here take a grassy track straight on beside a line of trees with wide views ahead. On reaching the golf course car park, follow the yellow lines marking the path across it. At the far side take a visible path straight on, aiming for the end of a hedge ahead. Here pass between the hedge and a single hawthorn bush to enter a hedged path. Take this straight on downhill, with the left-hand hedge giving way to an overgrown downland field at one point, before you pass through a belt of scrub to reach a squeeze-stile leading to a narrow macadam lane. Take this lane straight on downhill to join a residential road called Canesworde Road at a bend, then follow this straight on for a third of a mile ignoring all branching roads. Where it finally bears left and becomes Kirby Road, turn right through green gates into a recreation ground and follow a macadam path across it to gates on the far side. Go through these then turn left into Bullpond Lane to reach your starting point.

WALK 21: Toddington

Length of Walk:	(A) 11.4 miles / 18.4 Km
	(B) 5.8 miles / 9.3 Km
Starting Point:	Public car park in Leighton Road, Toddington.
Grid Ref:	TL008288

Maps: OS Landranger Sheet 166
OS Pathfinder Sheet TL02/12

How to get there / Parking: Toddington, 4.5 miles north of Dunstable, may be reached by leaving the M1 at Junction 12 (Toddington) and taking the A5120 towards Toddington and Dunstable. On reaching the village green known as Market Square, turn right following signs to the free car park.

Notes: As the car park closes at 7pm, if in doubt that you will complete the walk in time, park instead in one of the nearby side-streets. At the time of writing, some paths on both walks are in poor condition and difficult to follow. Also heavy nettle growth may be encountered in places in summer, particularly on path SL4 and bridleway HA21.

Today Toddington is probably best known for its M1 service area, but the village on its hilltop little more than a mile away with its church, pubs and cottages ranged around a picturesque green seems like a different world. In the past Toddington would seem to have been a place of some importance as it has an old town hall and its green is known as Market Square recalling the fact that it was once a market town. Its cruciform thirteenth-century church was lavishly renovated and extended in the fifteenth century when the wool trade had made the town rich. Inside this church is the Wentworth Chapel where Henrietta Maria Wentworth was buried in 1686. Born at Toddington in 1657, she became mistress of the Duke of Monmouth, first natural son of Charles II, who unsuccessfully attempted to overthrow James II in 1685 and was subsequently executed. Just to the east of the church is Conger Hill, a twelfth-century flat-topped castle motte which provides superb views across the Flit valley to a part of the Chiltern escarpment known as the

Barton Hills. The name 'Conger' is believed to be a corruption of 'conynger' meaning a 'rabbit warren'.

Both walks commence by crossing the village green and passing Conger Hill before traversing the Flit valley with wide views and climbing the Chiltern escarpment to Upper Sundon. Walk A then explores the quiet rolling hills to the north of Luton and visits Streatley (pronounced 'Strettley') before descending the escarpment, rejoining Walk B and returning to Toddington.

Both walks start from the car park in Leighton Road, Toddington, turn left out of it and follow this road, ignoring branching roads to the right, to reach the A5120. By the 'Bell' cross the A5120 and bear slightly right into Market Square, passing the church and the 'Oddfellows Arms' and entering Conger Lane. By a garage with large green doors facing you, turn left through a kissing-gate and fork half right onto path TD42 across the field, passing just right of the castle mound known as Conger Hill and its moat, then bearing slightly left to a gate and kissing-gate in the far corner of the field. Go through the kissing-gate and take bridleway TD43, a fenced track past a cemetery with fine views of the Barton Hills ahead. Now ignore a branching track to your left and take a grassy track straight on across fields. Where the left-hand side of the track becomes a ditch, keep right of it and follow it. By a small tree and the start of a left-hand fence, leave the ditch and go straight on across a field heading just left of a double-pole pylon to reach a fence gap onto the B579.

Cross this road and take a farm track (path TD45, later TD47) straight on ignoring the branching drive to Cowbridge Farm to your left. Having crossed a culvert over the River Flit, follow a left-hand ditch straight on to the near corner of Woodcock Wood. Here turn left crossing the ditch, then turn right and follow the outside edge of the wood uphill. At the top corner of the wood follow a line of trees straight on across the field to the right-hand end of Hipsey Spinney. Go straight on past this wood, then continue to a hedge gap ahead where you cross some rails and a culvert. Now bear slightly right heading for the right-hand of two hills ahead to reach the near corner of a wiggle in the hedge flanking the M1. Here go through the frame of an old kissing-gate and take a path through scrubland to another kissing-gate frame leading to a bridge over the M1. Turn left over this bridge then follow a concrete farm road. Where the concrete ends, bear slightly left to cross a railway footbridge, then take path SU2, a sunken lane, straight on uphill. On reaching a macadam road, follow it straight on uphill between old overgrown chalk quarries for over a third of a mile. After the road levels out, where it bears right, leave it, going straight on between bollards into a narrow macadam lane which soon becomes a village street at Upper Sundon. At a T-junction by the 'Crown', bear slightly left into Harlington Road and follow it to the 'Red Lion'. Now **Walk A** omits the next paragraph.

By the 'Red Lion' **Walk B** turns left between the far side of the pub and Sundon Stores & Post Office into bridleway SU3, a green lane, eventually reaching gates into a field. Now follow a grassy track straight on. After some 350 yards, just before the gates of a sewage works, fork right through a bridlegate by a field gate and cross a field diagonally to a bridlegate just left of its far corner. Go through this and take the obvious bridleway downhill along the inside edge of scrubland for a quarter mile eventually emerging into a field with a fine view ahead towards Harlington village on its low hill. Here turn left onto bridleway HA21, a grassy track following the left-hand hedge turning right at a corner of the field. Where the track turns right, leave it and follow the left-hand hedge straight on, rejoining **Walk A**. Now omit the next six paragraphs.

Just past the 'Red Lion', **Walk A** turns right onto path SU5 along the far edge of the green then between a pond and garden fences to a stile. Now go straight on across a field heading towards a tall pylon in the valley ahead. By the end of a sporadic hedge, turn left onto path SU14 along the near side of this hedge to reach a stile. Cross this, soon entering the 'White Hart' car park, and take its drive straight on out to Streatley Road. Turn right onto this road, then at a sharp left-hand bend, leave the road and take path SU11 following a right-hand hedge straight on for a third of a mile to Manor Road on the edge of Lower Sundon. Although having only a couple of farms and a few cottages, Lower Sundon can boast a large thirteenth-century church with mediaeval wall paintings and stone seats around its walls for the infirm from the time before pews were provided. In the seventeenth century this church was the scene of the wedding between William Foster, a persecutor of the non-conformist preacher John Bunyan, and Anne Wingate, sister of the magistrate who had Bunyan imprisoned at Bedford Gaol.

Turn right onto this road, then after some 30 yards, turn left through a hedge gap onto path SU12 to reach a junction of farm roads. Here take a farm road straight on for a third of a mile, soon passing Sundon Wood. At the far side of the wood, where the farm road turns left, bear slightly right, soon joining and following the left side of a hedge to the valley bottom, with views of Galley Hill, Warden Hill and part of Luton opening out ahead. Here turn left and follow a right-hand ditch and hedge. After some 80 yards, turn right over a footbridge onto path SL5, then turn left and follow a left-hand hedge for three-quarters of a mile, at one point turning right and then left and eventually climbing to reach a wiggle in the hedge near George Wood. (N.B. At the time of writing, the footbridge is missing but has been promised by the County Council. Should it not yet be in place, continue along the north side of the hedge to George Wood.) Here bear half right across the field to join and follow the left side of a winding sporadic tree belt, now with closer views of Galley Hill and Warden Hill to your left. At the far end of the tree belt bear half left across the field to the right-hand corner of the fence of a modern hospice. Here bear half left and follow the fence, then where it ends, bear slightly left across wasteground to a road junction near the entrance to the hospice.

Here cross the hospice drive and take path SL4, a track following the hospice fence into a field. Where the fence turns left, leave it and bear slightly left across the field to the corner of a hedge just right of a pylon. Keep left of this hedge and follow it to a corner of George Wood, then go through a gap and follow a left-hand hedge through four fields. At the far end of the fourth field, cross a stile and bear half right across a field heading just left of a thatched cottage at Streatley to cross a stile just right of the end of a hedge. Here bear slightly left across the next field to cross a stile at the far side, then continue through scrubland to Sharpenhoe Road at Streatley.

Turn left onto this road, then immediately left again into Bury Lane (path SL11). Take this lane past some cottages to a gate and stile then continue to a second gate. Here turn right through a gate and follow a grassy track uphill beside a right-hand hedge. Where the track turns right into Middle Farm, leave it and take a grassy path straight on to a stile into an alleyway. On reaching the end of a cul-de-sac road, cross it and take an alleyway straight on to a gate into Streatley churchyard. The fourteenth-century church with its fifteenth-century tower has a thirteenth-century font and a mediaeval wall painting of St. Catherine. In ruins for half a century, the church was thoroughly restored by Sir Albert Richardson in 1938.

Do not go through the churchyard gate, but turn left into another alleyway (path SL12) to Sundon Road, then turn right onto its narrow pavement. At a road junction, fork left onto the left-hand pavement of Sharpenhoe Road, then at the far end of the houses, turn left down some steps onto enclosed path SL13. By the gates to a radio station, go straight on through a gate into a field and follow its right-hand hedge. After some 200 yards turn right through a hedge gap and take path SU15 beside a right-hand hedge to enter a wood at the far side of the field, where you join the reverse direction of Walk 22.

In the wood turn left onto path SL15 skirting the top of the escarpment with views through the trees to your right. Where the path forks, keep right, descending and ignoring branching paths to your right, then climbing again, disregarding all branching and crossing paths. Now follow the inside edge of the wood, soon bearing left and ignoring a branching path to your right. At the top of a rise in an area of tall beeches, turn right onto worn path SU10 downhill. On leaving the wood where fine views open out ahead towards Harlington and Ampthill beyond, take path HA6 straight on downhill through scrub to a stile. Cross this and bear half left across a field to the left-hand end of a copse. Here do not go through the hedge gap, but bear half left (leaving Walk 22 again) and take bridleway HA20 following the left side of a hedge for a quarter mile. Where the hedge turns right, follow it, eventually reaching a hedge gap leading to a road. Turn left onto this road, then at a road junction turn right and almost immediately left onto bridleway HA21 following a grassy track beside a left-hand hedge. After a third of a mile, where the hedge ends, follow the track bearing right and passing a plantation and farm buildings to your right. At a T-junction of tracks, turn left and follow a track to reach a hedge ahead where you turn right and rejoin **Walk B**.

Walks A and B now follow the hedge, soon turning right, then just before the hedge turns left, turn left over a bridge and follow a winding hedged bridleway for a quarter mile. On emerging into a field near a bridge under the railway, bear half left onto path TD55 passing under this bridge, then turn right to reach a pylon. Here turn left through a hedge gap and bear slightly left across a field to a pylon in the middle of the field, then go straight on heading for a barn at Mill Farm beyond the M1. On joining a farm track at a bend, follow its winding course for a quarter mile to Old Park Farm. Here, at a junction of tracks, turn left onto path TD54 keeping left of the buildings. Then bearing right, soon joining and bearing left onto a macadam drive, follow this over the River Flit and the M1. At the far side of the motorway, ignore a branching road to the left, then after about 70 yards turn left onto a rough track through a hedge gap into a field. Follow the right-hand hedge straight on for some 200 yards then turn right over a footbridge and two stiles and go straight across a field to a stile and footbridge by a gate in the corner of the field leading to the B579. Cross this road and take path TD42 straight on through a gate following a right-hand hedge to cross a stile. Now take the fenced path straight on uphill with views opening out to your left. After passing a copse, where the fenced path turns right, climb over the left-hand fence and go through a hedge gap, then head for an electricity pole left of Toddington Church to rejoin your outward route by the corner of the cemetery. Here bear half right onto fenced bridleway TD43 and retrace your steps into Toddington.

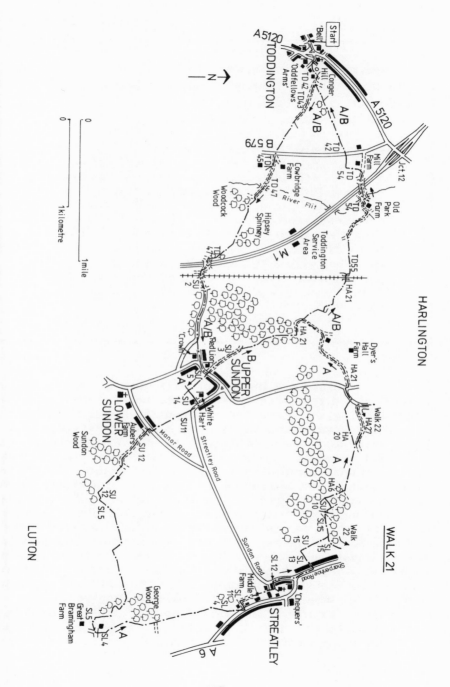

WALK 21

HARLINGTON

LUTON

Start

A 5120
TODDINGTON
A 5120

Jct.12

B 579

Mill Farm

Old Park Farm

Cowbridge Farm

Woodcock Wood

River Flit

Hipsey Spinney

Toddington Service Area

M1

TD 55

HA 21

Dyer's Hall Farm

UPPER SUNDON

'Crown'

'Red Lion'

'White Hart'

Manor Road

Streatley Road

LOWER SUNDON

Auber's Farm

Sundon Wood

Sundon Road

Walk 22

HA 20

HA 21

Walk 22

Sharpenhoe Road

Middle Farm

'Chequers'

STREATLEY

George Wood

Great Bramingham Farm

A 6

'Bell'

Conger Hill

'Oddfellows Arms'

N →

0 ____ 1 kilometre

0 ____ 1 mile

117

WALK 22: Harlington (Beds.)

Length of Walk: 6.0 miles / 9.7 Km

Starting Point: Harlington Village Hall car park.

Grid Ref: TL037304

Maps: OS Landranger Sheet 166
OS Pathfinder Sheets TL02/12 & TL03/13

How to get there / Parking: Harlington, 5.5 miles north of Dunstable, may be reached by leaving the M1 at Junction 12 (Toddington) and taking the A5120 towards Ampthill. After half a mile turn right onto a road signposted to Harlington Station and follow it to a crossroads in the village. Here turn right into Sundon Road where there is a car park by the village hall on your left.

Notes: When walked, this route was obstructed in several places, but it is hoped Bedfordshire County Council will secure the removal of most obstructions prior to publication.

Harlington, on a gault foothill of the Chilterns capped by its prominent thirteenth-century church, both catches the eye when looking out from the escarpment and provides fine views back towards the escarpment. Although the village with its station and close proximity to an M1 junction, has expanded considerably in recent years, this largely goes unnoticed when looking from the Chilterns as most of the new development is on the far side of the hill. In addition to its church, Harlington can also boast a number of attractive timber-framed and thatched cottages, but possibly its greatest claim to fame is its seventeenth-century manor house, one-time home of the magistrate Francis Wingate, who had the non-conformist preacher John Bunyan arrested at nearby Lower Samshill and brought to his house in Harlington, where he was imprisoned for the night and tried before being sent to Bedford Gaol where he wrote his 'Pilgrim's Progress'.

The walk, to which the view from the village positively invites you, takes you from Harlington across the valley and up the Chiltern escarpment near Streatley before leading you onto the outcrop of Sharpenhoe Clappers, with its superb views along the escarpment and out into the lowlands, descending to Sharpenhoe village and returning to Harlington.

Starting from the car park by Harlington Village Hall opposite the 'Carpenters Arms', turn right onto Sundon Road. At the village crossroads, turn right into Church Road, then at a bend by the church, fork right onto macadam path HA27 across the recreation ground. On joining Barton Road, turn right and after some 40 yards turn right again through a hedge gap onto path HA6 following the outside edge of a copse with fine views of the escarpment ahead. Where the copse ends, take a winding crop-break generally straight on, keeping right of a ditch when it commences, then ignoring a bridge over it and continuing until you reach a footbridge in front of you. Cross this and then head for a gap in trees on the skyline until you reach a field boundary. Here bear half left, keeping right of a hedge and following it to a footbridge leading to a road.

Turn right onto this road, then after a quarter mile at a right-hand bend, turn left through gates onto bridleway HA27 following a winding track. On nearing a left-hand copse, turn right through a hedge gap, then bear half left onto path HA6 (joining the reverse direction of Walk 21) crossing a large field to a stile into scrubland at the top of the second rise to your left. Cross this stile and a crossing path and follow path HA6 steeply uphill through scrub to an area of open downland where a seat gives you an opportunity to rest and admire the view across the lowlands behind you towards Harlington and Ampthill.

Now take path SU10 straight on uphill into mature beechwoods. At the far side of the wood, turn left and follow a path hugging the inside edge of the wood until reaching the end of a handrail. Here at a three-way fork, take the centre option (path SL15), then at a second fork, keep left and go straight on uphill to the top of the escarpment. Now follow the top edge of the escarpment through the wood until the path turns right and leaves the wood. Turn left here (leaving Walk 21 again) and follow the outside edge of the wood until you reach some gates. Go through these and continue to follow the edge of the wood to a bulge in it where you strike out across the field to a hedge gap opposite. Here climb a fence and descend a steep bank carefully, then cross Sharpenhoe Road and take path SL14 straight on through a squeeze-stile beside a gate onto a macadam track. Where the track forks, keep right passing through a gate. Now follow the outside edge of a wood bearing left and entering scrubland. On emerging onto Sharpenhoe Clappers, a superb view opens out to your left and ahead.

Here take an obvious path beside a left-hand fence straight on, soon joining the earthworks of an Iron Age camp with a wood to your right. Where the fence turns left and the main path turns right, fork left off it and take a flight of steps down the steep hill. At the bottom cross a stile and follow a left-hand hedge straight on to reach a road. Turn left onto this and follow it into Sharpenhoe village.

Sharpenhoe, at the foot of the Clappers, has always been a hamlet of the hilltop village of Streatley. Apart from sharing its name, meaning 'steep hill', with the hill from which it derives, Sharpenhoe's other claim to fame is linked to the former moated manor, of which only the moat survives just to the east of Bury Farm. This house was home to both the sixteenth-century playwright Thomas Norton, a forerunner of and a model for Shakespeare and Marlowe, who was buried at Streatley in 1584 and the leading seventeenth-century mathematician, Edmund Wingate.

At a road junction by 'The Lynmore', turn right onto bridleway SL19, the drive to Bury Farm. Just past a left-hand house, wiggle slightly to your right and continue through a farmyard, passing left of some large barns onto a wide field track. After a third of a mile, on reaching a crossing power-line, turn left under the power-line onto bridleway SL18, crossing a ditch (N.B. if there is no bridge, use a culvert about 30 yards further north) and then following a left-hand ditch and the edge of a wood called Sharpenhoe Grove. At the far end of the wood, go straight on across the field, heading for a white house called Grange Farm to cross a rail-stile in the next hedge. Now go straight on, aiming for gateposts capped by large white balls to pass through this gateway and reach Harlington Road.

Turn right onto this road, then after a few yards, turn left through a hedge gap onto path SL16 and follow a right-hand hedge to the far end of the field. Now follow the hedge to the left for a few yards, then by a small ash tree, ignore a bridge over the brook to your right and cross a shallow ditch by the tree into the next field. Here continue to follow the right-hand hedge, wiggling to your right at one point, until you reach a footbridge in the hedge. Turn right across this onto path HA5. Now turn left and follow a left-hand ditch, ignoring a footbridge across it and soon turning right. At the far end of the field, follow the hedge round to the right, then turn left over a footbridge at the end of the hedge to reach a road.

Here bear half left across the road and a culvert onto path HA18, then turn right and follow a right-hand ditch and hedge. At a corner of the field, go straight on through a hedge gap, then turn left and follow a left-hand hedge. Where the hedge ends, cross a small ditch and (temporarily rejoining your outward route) turn right onto path HA6, soon bearing left. Where the right-hand ditch bears right, leave HA6

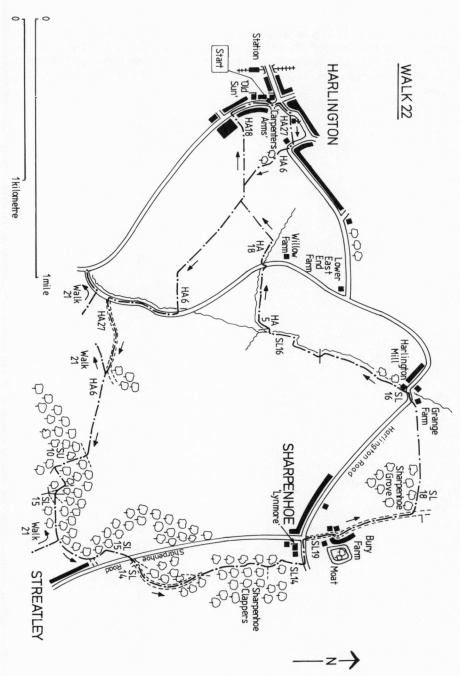

WALK 22

HARLINGTON

Start

Station

'Old Sun'

Carpenters Arms'

HA27

HA6

HA18

Lower East End Farm

Willow Farm

HA 18

HA6

Walk 21

HA27

Walk 21

HA6

HA 5

SL16

Harlington Mill

SL 16

Grange Farm

Sharpenhoe Grove

SL 18

SU 10

SL 15

Walk 21

SHARPENHOE

'Lynmore'

Harlington Road

SL19

Bury Farm

Moat

SL14

Sharpenhoe Clappers

SL 15

Sharpenhoe Road

SL 14

STREATLEY

N →

0

1 kilometre

0

1 mile

121

and take path HA18 straight on across the field to a group of trees right of some houses on the skyline and left of the field corner. By these trees enter a hedged path past back gardens leading to Sundon Road. Turn right onto this passing the 'Old Sun' to reach your starting point.

WALK 23: Barton-le-Clay

Length of Walk: 6.8 miles / 11.0 Km
Starting Point: Barton-le-Clay Church.
Grid Ref: TL085304
Maps: OS Landranger Sheet 166
OS Pathfinder Sheets TL02/12 & TL03/13

How to get there / Parking: Barton-le-Clay, 6 miles north of Luton, may be reached from the town by taking the A6 towards Bedford. After about 5 miles, fork left onto the B655 towards Hitchin. On reaching the village, turn right, (still on the B655), then, at the second sharp left-hand bend, turn right into Church Road and find a suitable parking space.

Barton-le-Clay, formerly known as Barton-in-the-Clay, sits astride the old route of the A6 from London to Bedford and the Northwest of England at the foot of the Chiltern escarpment and as such, in the days of the stagecoach, was a place of busy coaching inns. Despite the village being swamped by modern housing in the 1960s and 1970s, the vicinity of its thirteenth-century church with its fifteenth-century tower and finely-carved roof depicting eagles, saints and apostles, its moated sixteenth-century rectory and a number of attractive cottages, remains an area of rural tranquility and beauty. For the walker, however, Barton's principal attraction is as a centre for walks with spectacular views of and from the range of hills which bears its name and represents the northern-most ridge in the Chilterns and which are thought to have been the inspiration for John Bunyan's 'delectable mountains' in 'Pilgrim's Progress'.

The walk, indeed, first takes you from Barton through arable fields below the escarpment, offering fine views of the hills, to the Hertfordshire village of Hexton, before climbing up a wooded combe to explore the hilltop plateau near the Icknield Way to the south. It then culminates by emerging at the top of a spectacular downland combe which it skirts before descending gently back into Barton.

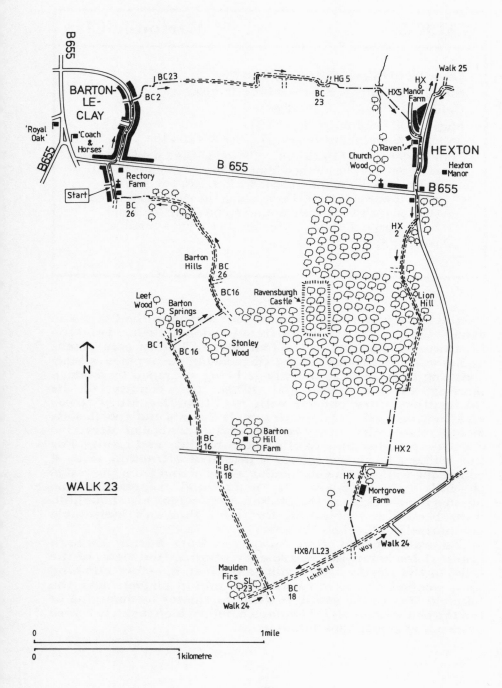

WALK 23

Starting from the entrance to Barton-le-Clay Church, take Church Road back to the B655. Here turn right, then immediately left into Manor Road, formerly known by the intriguing name of Rogues Lane. After a third of a mile, just past house no. 113 ('Oakengates'), turn right between safety barriers onto path BC2. Take this enclosed macadam path to a footbridge, then turn left with fine views of the hills to your right and follow a left-hand hedge to a field corner where you turn right. After about 70 yards, turn left through a hedge gap, then turn right onto path BC23 following a right-hand hedge straight on. Where the hedge ends, take a grassy track straight on with Shillington Church coming into view on a hilltop to your left. On reaching the end of a hedge, keep right of it, then, at its far end, follow the grassy track turning left then right. Now follow a right-hand hedge, eventually wiggling to the right, to reach a corner of the field. Here go straight on through a hedge gap and take path HG5 following a right-hand hedge to a footbridge into Hertfordshire at the far end of the field. Cross this, then bear half right onto path HX5, crossing the field diagonally to reach a road by the right-hand end of a row of bungalows at Hexton.

The village of Hexton, in a salient of Hertfordshire surrounded on three sides by Bedfordshire, has traditionally been an estate village. Before the First World War, it was almost completely rebuilt by the then Lord of the Manor, George Hodgson. Earlier owners of the Manor, Caroline Young and her French émigré husband, Joseph de Lautour, as well as adding two wings to the eighteenth-century Manor, built a new village school and village pump and also partially rebuilt the twelfth-century church. Two sides of its fifteenth-century tower, which was not rebuilt at this period, collapsed in 1947 and since then the tower has remained a ruin.

Turn right onto the road into the village and at a T-junction, turn right again following the village street past the 'Raven' and a high wall surrounding Hexton Manor to reach a crossroads by the ornate village pump. Here cross the B655 and take the Lilley road straight on. After some 200 yards, at a left-hand bend, fork right through a gate onto path HX2 and take this green lane straight on. Where its hedges end, follow the track straight on to a fork where you keep left and take a grassy track steeply uphill between woods. At the top of the hill, follow the grassy track straight on along the outside edge of the right-hand wood. At the far end of the field go straight on through a hedge gap, then turn right, still following the outside edge of the wood. After some 80 yards, at a corner of the field, turn left and follow the left side of a hedge for a third of a mile to a hedge gap ahead leading to a road. Turn right onto this road, then, just past the end of a tree belt, turn left through white gates onto bridleway HX1, the macadam drive to Mortgrove Farm. At the farm, follow the drive straight on past the buildings, then go straight on through a gap between gates and follow a right-hand fence, later a hedge, straight on for a quarter mile to the Icknield Way (HX8/LL23).

Turn right onto this Ancient British green road named after Boadicea's people, the Iceni, (joining the reverse direction of Walk 24) and follow it (later as BC18) for nearly half a mile towards Galley Hill, believed to be a corruption of 'Gallows Hill' as the remains of fifteenth-century gallows victims have been found in an older barrow there. Where a tree belt begins to your right, turn right onto a grassy track beside a right-hand hedge (leaving Walk 24 again) and follow it (still BC18) for two-thirds of a mile through two fields, with wide views to your left towards Luton and Streatley at the top of the first rise.

On reaching a road, turn left onto it, then, after about 150 yards, turn right onto bridleway BC16, a stony track beside a right-hand hedge. Where, after a quarter mile, the hedge ends, continue to follow the track bearing slightly left across a field with views towards lowland Bedfordshire opening out ahead. At the far side of the field, ignore a branching bridleway to your right and follow the track (now path BC1) straight on for about 30 yards, then turn right over a stile into scrubland onto path BC15 and immediately fork right onto path BC19, soon crossing another stile. Now follow a right-hand hedge straight on past the top of a steep combe, at the foot of which are Barton Springs. At the far end of the field, turn left and follow a right-hand fence to a gate and stile in it. Cross the stile and continue along a stony track on the other side of the fence (bridleway BC16 again), passing the top of another part of the combe and Ravensburgh Castle, a 22-acre Iron Age hill fort in woods half a mile to your right. At a fork, take bridleway BC26, a grassy track, straight on over the brow of the hill, then descending and swinging left round the face of the hill, at one point passing an old chalkpit. Where the track ends in a field, turn right and then bear left to follow a right-hand hedge, soon with a fence to your left, to reach the end of Church Road. Here turn right for your starting point.

WALK 24: Lilley (Treasures Grove Picnic Area)

Length of Walk: 7.4 miles / 11.9 Km

Starting Point: Northeast end of Treasures Grove Picnic Area on the Icknield Way north of Lilley.

Grid Ref: TL109283

Maps: OS Landranger Sheet 166
OS Pathfinder Sheet TL02/12

How to get there / Parking: Treasures Grove Picnic Area, 4.5 miles north of Luton, may be reached from the town by taking the A505 towards Hitchin. 1 mile beyond the edge of the town, fork left onto a road signposted to Great Offley, Lilley and Kings Walden. At a T-junction, turn left onto the Lilley and Hexton road and follow this winding road for over 2 miles passing through Lilley and eventually reaching Treasures Grove Picnic Area in front of you at a sharp left-hand bend.

Treasures Grove Picnic Area, on the ancient Icknield Way near Lilley, might perhaps be expected to be a site where buried treasure had been found, but in fact it is named after an official of Hertfordshire County Council which created the picnic area. The village of Lilley, visited in the course of the walk, is clearly recognisable as an old estate village with a large number of its cottages bearing the lion rampant crest of the Docwra family (pronounced 'Dockray') of nearby Putteridge Bury. In the seventeenth century, Lilley was a centre of non-conformity being home to the religious writer, James Janeway, and it is believed that John Bunyan, author of 'Pilgrim's Progress', secretly preached in the cellar of one of the village cottages. An infamous later resident of the village was the nineteenth-century alchemist Johann Kellerman who disappeared from Lilley as suddenly as he came.

The walk, which includes a series of fine views, first leads you from Treasures Grove along the Icknield Way to near Telegraph Hill where a slight detour up the hill is rewarded by a magnificent view. You now turn across a plateau called Lilley Hoo, the site of an eighteenth-century racecourse frequented by King George IV, then continue by way of Lilley to Butterfield Green and the fine chalk downs and viewpoints

WALK 24

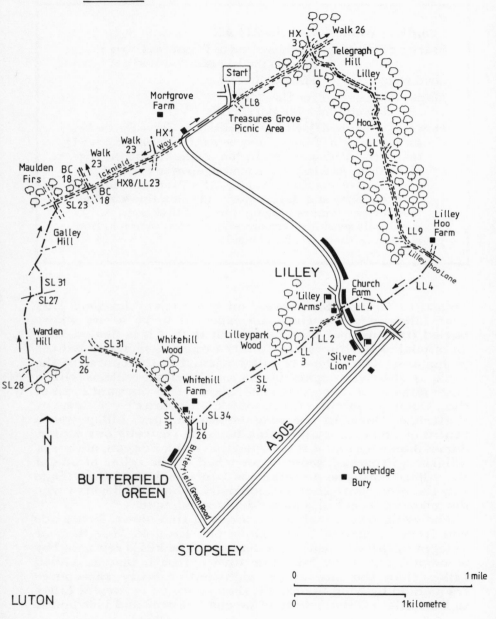

of Warden Hill and Galley Hill near the edge of Luton before returning along the Icknield Way to Treasures Grove.

Starting from the rear end of Treasures Grove Picnic Area, go through a gap by a gate and follow the wide grassy Icknield Way (LL8) straight on towards Telegraph Hill. After a quarter mile the Way becomes tree-lined, then, after a further quarter mile at a fork, keep right. If wishing to see the extensive view of lowland Bedfordshire from the hilltop, go straight on up the hill. Otherwise, fork immediately right again onto bridleway LL9, a grassy track uphill into a copse. At the far side of the copse, continue to follow a winding grassy track uphill to reach a tumulus to your right. (N.B. From here to Lilleyhoo Lane the described route differs slightly from the official line of the bridleway which is currently undefined and impossible to describe with any accuracy. Should the official line be re-established and marked, walkers should heed the waymarking.) Just past the tumulus, follow the track bearing half left across a field at the northern end of Lilley Hoo, heading towards a radio mast on the skyline to reach the corner of a hedge by a V-shaped oak tree. Here bear half right following a winding right-hand hedge for some 350 yards. Just before a powerline, where the hedge turns right, leave it and follow the grassy track straight on across a field to join the outside edge of a copse. Now follow this track straight on alongside the copse, then a larger wood, ignoring branching tracks to left and right. At the far end of the wood take the track straight on across a field to the corner of a hedge then beside the left-hand hedge to enter a green lane called Lilleyhoo Lane. Follow this lane straight on downhill with views towards Great Offley ahead to reach a bend in a macadam road near Lilley Hoo Farm.

Take this road straight on for 30 yards then turn right through a hedge gap onto path LL4. Now follow a right-hand hedge straight on for nearly half a mile over the top of a hill with wide views of Lilley Bottom ahead and to your left. At the far end of the field, cross a stile and bear half right across the next field, heading just right of some barns at Church Farm to a stile. Cross this and go straight across a field heading left of Lilley Church to reach the near left-hand corner of a fenced orchard, then follow the orchard fence straight on to a stile. Here continue between hedges to Lilley village street near the church, where you turn left.

Lilley Church was almost completely rebuilt in 1871 by Thomas Jekyll, but retains the chancel arch of its twelfth-century predecessor together with some lavish monuments to members of the Docwra family.

After some 50 yards, turn right onto path LL2 into the car park of the Cassell Memorial Hall, following its right-hand hedge into a green lane. Where this lane turns right, leave it and go straight on into a field following its right-hand hedge (later on path LL3) past Lilleypark Wood. At the far end of the field, go straight on through a gap in the county boundary hedge and take path SL34 straight on uphill, passing just left of a single oak tree near the top and continuing to a hedge gap left of Whitehill Farm. Here cross a stile and bear slightly left towards a distant barn, crossing a field diagonally to another stile, then take path LU26 straight on to a stile under an ash tree leading to Butterfield Green Road.

Turn right onto this road and where it forks, go left onto bridleway SL31, a wide farm road with extensive views opening across Luton to your left and towards Warden Hill ahead. After passing Whitehill Wood to your right, at a crossways go straight on for a further quarter mile. At a right-hand bend, fork left onto path SL26, following a sporadic left-hand hedge and later a line of trees, swinging left and descending. At the bottom corner of the field, turn right and on reaching the corner of an area of scrubland on Warden Hill, ignore a hedge gap to your left, then turn left onto a path into the scrub keeping the line of trees to your left. After some 300 yards, where the tall trees to your left end, look out for indistinct path SL28 to your right. Turn right onto this and follow its winding course steeply uphill to the top of Warden Hill, where panoramic views open out over Luton and towards the back of the Chiltern escarpment ahead.

Here turn right onto a worn path, then, ignoring crossing paths, bear slightly left and follow the worn path along the ridge just left of its crest. At the far end of the ridge, the path gradually swings to the right and descends to reach fenced bridleway SL27 in a dip. Turn right onto this, then, where the left-hand fence ends, turn left rejoining bridleway SL31 and following the left-hand fence gradually swinging left. At a corner of the field, ignore a gate and a stile in the fence and turn right, still following the fence up Galley Hill, the name of which is believed to be a corruption of 'Gallows Hill', as the remains of fifteenth-century gallows victims as well as fourth-century and neolithic corpses have been found in one of the ancient barrows scattered across the hill.

On reaching a gate in front of you, go through it, disregarding a branching path to your right, and continue through patchy scrub over the top of Galley Hill and one of the barrows, then descend gradually to a bridlegate leading onto a golf course. Here look to your right to check that no golfer is driving towards you, then go straight on across a fairway to a gap right of two small silver birches. Now follow a right-hand hedge straight on past a green to a chalky track, onto which you turn left to reach a hedge gap leading to the Icknield Way.

Turn right into this ancient green lane (SL23) and follow it (later as BC18, then HX8/LL23) straight on for three-quarters of a mile, joining the reverse direction of Walk 23 at the first crossways, later leaving it again and eventually emerging through a gap by a gate onto a bend in the Hexton road. Now follow this road straight on to your starting point.

WALK 25:   Pegsdon (North)

Length of Walk: 7.9 miles / 12.8 Km

Starting Point: Entrance to cul-de-sac road at Pegsdon
village green.

Grid Ref: TL118302

Maps: OS Landranger Sheet 166
OS Pathfinder Sheet TL03/13

How to get there / Parking: Pegsdon, 4 miles west of
Hitchin, may be reached from the town by taking the
B655 towards Barton-le-Clay and following it for 4 miles,
then turning right into a road signposted to Pegsdon and
Shillington. After less than 100 yards, turn left into a
wide cul-de-sac road where you can park.

Pegsdon, a tiny village with a green and a pub at the foot of
the Chiltern escarpment below Deacon Hill, has always been a
hamlet of the Bedfordshire parish of Shillington surrounded
on three sides by Hertfordshire. In contrast, its mother village
of Shillington, which is visited in the course of this walk, with
its prominent hilltop church and a wealth of attractive brick
cottages gives the impression of having once been a place of
some importance.

The walk, by Chiltern standards one of a very easy nature
for its length, involving only one climb of any significance,
keeps criss-crossing the county boundary, first leading you
along the foot of the hills to the Hertfordshire village of
Hexton. You then strike out across the lowlands with wide
views to reach the Bedfordshire village of Shillington and its
vantage point of Church Hill. From here it continues with
more wide views to the Hertfordshire village of Pirton with its
picturesque cottages and Norman church and castle
earthworks before returning over the escarpment outcrop of
Knocking Hoe with its superb views of the lowlands to
Pegsdon.

Starting from the entrance to the cul-de-sac road on Pegsdon village
green, take the Shillington road and follow it for a quarter mile, then
turn left into a cul-de-sac road to Bury Farm and some cottages. Just

past the farm, where its macadam surface ends, take its rough continuation (bridleway SH4) straight on, soon joining the edge of a tree belt and bearing right. At a signposted junction at the far end of the tree belt, turn left, still following the rough road beside the tree belt. On passing an old watermill known as Hexton Mill, where you enter Hertfordshire, the road called Mill Lane becomes macadamed again. Now follow it for a further half mile, wiggling left at one point, then turning sharp left to reach the edge of Hexton.

At a left-hand bend about 100 yards short of the start of Hexton village, turn sharp right onto path HX6, heading for the right-hand side of a gap between low tree belts ahead, with views of Higham Gobion's fourteenth-century church on a hilltop to your left and Shillington Church on a hilltop to your right and later the escarpment behind you. After over half a mile, on reaching the end of a thick hedge to your right, take a grassy track beside a right-hand ditch straight on. Where the track and ditch bear left, go straight on over a sleeper footbridge and head for the left-hand end of a hedge ahead. Here cross a ditch marking the county boundary and turn right onto path SH18, following a right-hand hedge and ditch, later a stream, to a field corner. Now turn left onto path SH19 following the right-hand hedge and stream for a further half mile through two fields. On nearing Chalkeybush Farm at Apsley End, the path bears slightly left away from the stream, soon joining a right-hand hedge and following it to cross a stile by a gate to reach a road.

Cross this and take path SH20 straight on between gardens to cross a stile. Now follow a left-hand fence straight on through a paddock. At the far end of the paddock, turn left over a stile and take path SH42 following a right-hand hedge and stream through two fields. In the second field, by a farm bridge over the stream, take path SH40 bearing half left across the field to cross a stile by a gate. Now turn right onto enclosed bridleway SH8, soon crossing a bridge to enter a field. Here follow the right-hand hedge straight on, soon with the wall of Shillington churchyard on your left, and climb a series of steps to reach the end of Church Street by the churchyard gate.

Shillington's early fourteenth-century stone church, with its tower rebuilt in brick in 1750 following the collapse of its old tower in 1701, is thought not to have been the first church on this hilltop site and indeed the discovery of ancient coins and Roman pottery on the hill indicates early human habitation. In any event, its elevated location suggests that in mediaeval times the site will have also served a military function as a look-out post.

Now take Church Street straight on. Just past the former village school, turn right onto path SH21, a macadamed alleyway called The Twitchel, and follow it downhill to High Road. Cross this road and a footbridge and stile opposite, then follow a right-hand fence straight on across a field to a stile. Here bear slightly right, heading just right of a gap between low tree belts ahead, with Pirton Church coming into view ahead, to reach a small culvert over a ditch. Cross this and turn right beside the ditch. In a corner of the field, turn left and follow a right-hand hedge through two fields. In the second field, where the hedge turns right, follow it and later a ditch to a field corner. Here go straight on through a thick hedge at the county boundary, crossing a culvert, then take path PI1 straight on, soon joining a left-hand hedge. Where this hedge turns left, leave it bearing slightly left over the top of a rise, where a fine view opens out towards Pirton ahead and the Chiltern escarpment to your right. When Pirton Church comes into view ahead, aim for it to reach a culvert in a hedge gap. Here bear slightly left, heading for the near end of a hedge ahead with views towards Holwell opening out to your left. By the end of the hedge, cross a culvert and follow a grassy track along the left side of the hedge. Where the hedge ends and the tracks turns right, leave it and go straight on, heading just right of the spike of Pirton Church (slightly concealed by poplar trees) to cross a stile in the far hedge. Now go straight on over the next field to a stile near a converted timber-framed barn leading to an alleyway. Go through the alleyway, then turn right into West Lane.

Almost immediately turn left by a thatched cottage into a rough lane (still path PI1) which soon narrows to a hedged path and continues past a right-hand field before going through an alleyway to reach the end of a road called Docklands. Go straight on along the road, then, at a T-junction, turn right into Crabtree Lane and almost immediately left onto a hedged macadam path which leads to Toot Hill, then bears left to the churchyard gate.

Toot Hill to your right represents the remains of a Norman motte and bailey castle with an exceptionally large moat built by Ralph de Limesi to command the Hitchin Gap. In the light of its Saxon name 'Toot' meaning 'look-out', it is clear, however, that the Saxons must have previously had a look-out post at this point. The nearby twelfth-century church, like that of Shillington, suffered a collapse of its tower in 1874 and so the present tower dates from its reconstruction in 1876.

By the churchyard gate, turn right onto path PI17, soon passing through a kissing-gate, then follow a right-hand fence across the meadow. Soon after the fence turns right by the corner of the moat, turn right onto worn path PI18 which leads to a kissing-gate into the end of a village street called Bury End. Follow this road bearing right, then, at a T-junction near the 'Cat and Fiddle', turn left. On reaching Hitchin Road, cross it and take hedged bridleway PI8 known as Wood

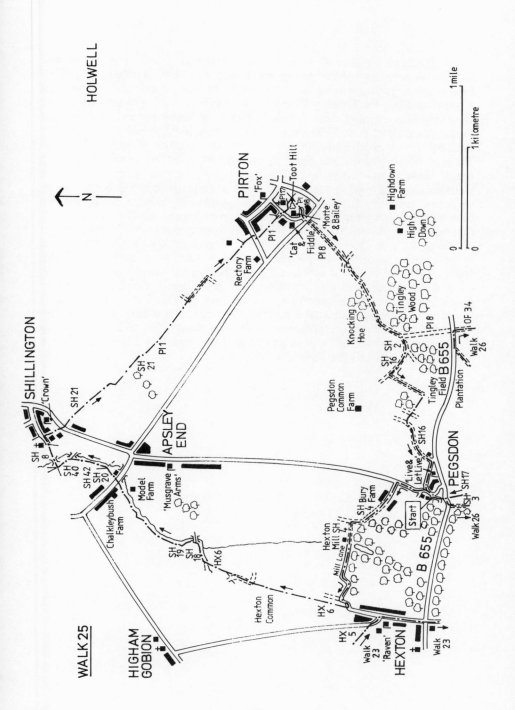

WALK 25

HOLWELL

← N →

SHILLINGTON

'Crown'
SH 8
SH 40
SH 42
SH 20
SH 21

HIGHAM GOBION

Chalkleybush Farm
Model Farm
'Musgrave Arms'
APSLEY END
SH 19
SH 18
HX 6

Hexton Common
HX
HX 6
Hexton Mill Mill Lane
SH Bury 4 Farm
SH 4
Mill Lane
HX 5
Walk 23
'Raven'
HEXTON
Walk 23

PIRTON
'Fox'
Toot Hill
PI 7
PI 18
PI 1
PI 1
'Cat & Fiddle'
PI 8
'Motte & Bailey'
Rectory Farm
SH 21
PI 11

Pegsdon Common Farm

Knocking Hoe
Tingley Wood
High Down
Highdown Farm
SH 16
SH 2
Tingley Field
B 655
Plantation
PI 8
Walk 26
OF 34
SH 16
'Live & Let Live'
SH 17
SH 17
PEGSDON
Start
B 655
Walk 26 3

Walk 23

0 _____ 1 mile
0 _____ 1 kilometre

135

Lane straight on for nearly a mile. After a third of a mile, the bridleway widens into a green road and starts to climb gently with hedge gaps giving views in places. At the top of the hill known as Knocking Hoe, by Tingley Wood to your left (a Viking name meaning 'meeting-place in a clearing'), where the lane opens out into a field and forks, turn right onto bridleway SH2, recrossing the county boundary and following a right-hand hedge. By the corner of a wood called Tingley Field Plantation, fork right onto path SH16, a winding farm track down the hillside offering superb views across lowland Bedfordshire. To your right, you pass a strange-looking combe with terraces, possibly the result of chalk quarrying, backed by Knocking Hoe which is capped by a Neolithic barrow known as Knocking Knoll due to ghostly knocking sounds said to emanate from it. On reaching a crossing hedge line, turn left onto a grassy track following the right-hand side of the hedge over two rises. At the far end of the field, turn right and follow a left-hand fence bounding an old chalk quarry, soon descending past a plantation to a green road. Cross this and go straight on through a hedge gap and across a field, then turn left onto a macadam farm road and follow it for a third of a mile to reach the end of Pegsdon village street near its junction with the B655. Turn right along the village street past the 'Live and Let Live', then, at a T-junction, turn left for your starting point.

WALK 26: Pegsdon (South)

Length of Walk: (A) 8.5 miles / 13.6 Km
                               (B) 2.1 miles / 3.4 Km
                               (C) 6.9 miles / 11.1 Km

Starting Points: (A/B) Entrance to cul-de-sac road at
                                    Pegsdon village green.
                               (C) Crossroads near 'Green Man',
                                      Great Offley.

Grid Refs: (A/B) TL118302 / (C) TL142271

Maps: OS Landranger Sheet 166
          OS Pathfinder Sheets TL02/12 & TL03/13

How to get there / Parking: (A/B) See Walk 25.
                                              (C) See Walk 27.

Pegsdon, described in Walk 25, at the foot of Deacon Hill and Telegraph Hill, with its good road access, pub and two highly scenic paths up the Chiltern escarpment, is an ideal starting point for walkers to climb and explore some of the finest and least spoilt downs in the whole Chiltern range.

Walks A and B indeed use both these paths to climb Telegraph Hill to the Icknield Way with fine views of the downs and the lowlands beneath; while Walks A and C take the Icknield Way past Deacon Hill and explore the quiet hills around Wellbury and Little Offley interspersed with further fine views across the hills and the Hitchin Gap.

Walks A and B start from the entrance to the cul-de-sac road on Pegsdon village green and lead you up the cul-de-sac to a right-hand bend. Here leave this road and go straight on, crossing a narrow strip of verge and the B655, then turn right along its far verge. At a right-hand bend, turn left through a bridlegate onto bridleway SH3, following a grassy track uphill along the outside edge of a tree belt with fine views of Deacon Hill to your left and later Telegraph Hill ahead. After nearly two-thirds of a mile, having crossed a rise, at a corner of the field fork right off the track through a hedge gap onto bridleway HX3. Now in Hertfordshire bear left and follow a grassy track beside a belt of scrub with views of Galley Hill and Warden Hill near Luton to your right. At the far side of the field, go straight on

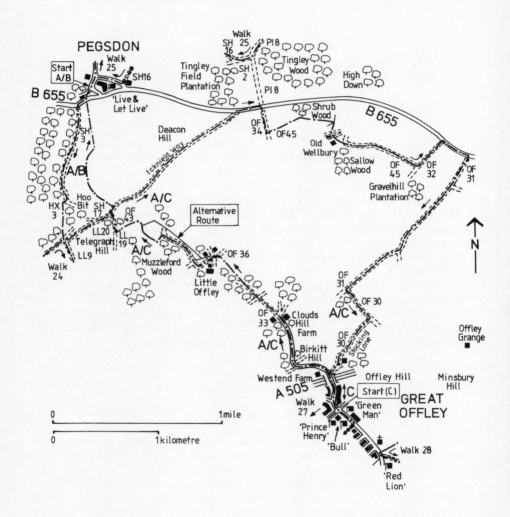

through a hedge gap onto the Ancient British Icknield Way, which at this point divides into several tracks due, no doubt, to the difficulties for horse-drawn vehicles of climbing Telegraph Hill. Cross the tree-lined lower route and go straight on through bushes to reach a parallel grass track. Turn left onto this, briefly joining the route of Walk 24, and follow the track up Telegraph Hill with fine views to your left and behind near the top. At the top of the hill, on reaching the corner of a field, take the grassy track straight on along the edge of the field rejoining the alternative routes of the Icknield Way. At the far side of the field, joining **Walk C**, go straight on into a tree-lined green lane.

After about 70 yards, **Walk B** turns left through a hedge gap onto path SH17. Now read the last paragraph. **Walks A and C** follow this ancient lane along the county boundary straight on for a mile past Deacon Hill with the tall dense hedges eventually giving way to lower ones and the trees petering out to give attractive views of the surrounding hills and lowlands to the north. On reaching a gate, go through a gap beside it and turn right onto the B655, following its generally walkable right-hand verge around a right-hand bend.

Now turn right onto bridleway OF34, a wide rough lane. After some 250 yards, by a tall oak tree, turn left through a hedge gap onto path OF45 heading for a smaller tree on the skyline with a view of High Down to your left. Go straight on past this tree to reach a hedge gap at the far side of the field then follow the outside edge of a plantation straight on. On reaching a corner of the plantation, bear half right across the field heading just right of the right-hand side of a group of trees ahead to reach the corner of a hedge. Here turn right and head for the left-hand end of the farmhouse at Old Wellbury to reach a farm road by the corner of a fence. Cross this road and follow the left-hand fence straight on downhill to cross a second farm road. Now bear half left uphill to reach a corner of the field by Sallow Wood. Here take a short green lane along the edge of the wood into a field, then follow a grassy track beside a left-hand hedge straight on downhill through two fields with fine views ahead towards Hitchin and Stevenage, eventually climbing again to reach a green lane (bridleway OF32). Turn left into this lane and follow it to the B655.

Turn right onto this road, then, after some 350 yards, turn right again onto bridleway OF31. Take this green lane straight on for three-quarters of a mile, climbing gently to the top of a ridge where views of Minsbury Hill and Offley Hill open out ahead, then continuing to the bottom of the hill. Here at a fork, go right and follow a grassy track beside a left-hand hedge. After over a third of a mile, on nearing a powerline, turn left into a branching green lane (bridleway OF30) and follow it for a quarter mile over a rise with wide views to your left. At another junction of green lanes turn right (still on OF30) and follow this sunken way called Stocking Lane uphill for a quarter mile. On emerging into a field with views towards the lowlands over your right shoulder, follow a grassy track beside a left-hand hedge straight on through two fields to join a macadam drive. Turn right onto this and follow it to School Lane at Birkitt Hill on the edge of Great Offley. Here **Walk A** turns right, while **Walk C** turns left and follows School Lane back into the village.

Walk C starts from the crossroads near the 'Green Man' at Great Offley (described in Walk 27) and takes School Lane for a quarter mile to cross the bridge over the A505. Now **Walks A and C** follow this quiet winding road for half a mile with views to your right towards Hitchin in places. At a fork by Clouds Hill Farm, take the left-hand option, macadamed bridleway OF33, straight on towards Little Offley, with its fine late Tudor brick manor house coming into view ahead. After entering an avenue of lime trees, at a left-hand bend, fork right off the macadam drive, following a left-hand hedge straight on. Having passed a cottage, turn left onto a crossing track (bridleway OF36) into a farmyard.

Now bear slightly right off the track and across the farmyard and take a track between two black buildings ahead. (From here for the next half mile the route follows a permissive path which can be closed at any time. Should this occur, an alternative route via public rights of way is indicated on the plan, but this tends to be difficult to follow.) Follow this track straight on past the back of Little Offley House, then, at a corner of the field, turning right. Where the track forks, take the right-hand option straight on beside a left-hand hedge, later the edge of Muzzleford Wood. At the far end of the wood turn left, still following its outside edge to a field corner, then turn right and follow a left-hand hedge. Where the hedge turns left, take bridleway OF43, still following the hedge to its end. Now go straight on, soon joining a right-hand hedge and continuing beside it to a field corner. Here take bridleway LL19 straight on through a hedge gap and across a field for about 40 yards to a crossing track. Turn right onto this, now on bridleway LL20, following it into and through a copse, then beside a right-hand hedge to the Icknield Way near Telegraph Hill.

Here **Walk C** turns right onto the Icknield Way. Now go back five paragraphs. **Walk A** also turns right onto the Icknield Way, rejoining **Walk B**, then, after about 70 yards, **Walks A and B** turn left through a hedge gap onto path SH17, re-entering Bedfordshire. Go straight on across a field to the corner of a hedge, then follow this right-hand hedge straight on with views through the hedge of a deep, steep-sided combe. At a corner of the field, go straight on into a belt of scrub, descending with views in places of the combe backed by Deacon Hill.

Eventually you re-emerge from the scrub and follow its outside edge straight on downhill with wide views. Where the scrubland ends, take a grassy path straight on over a rise, then downhill to a squeeze stile leading to the B655 opposite your starting point.

WALK 27: Great Offley

Length of Walk:	6.8 miles / 11.0Km
Starting Point:	Crossroads near 'Green Man', Great Offley.
Grid Ref:	TL142271

Maps: OS Landranger Sheet 166
OS Pathfinder Sheet TL02/12

How to get there / Parking: Great Offley, 3 miles southwest of Hitchin, may be reached from the town by taking the A505 towards Luton for 2 miles, then forking left onto a road signposted to Great Offley, Lilley and Kings Walden. At the village crossroads, turn left into the High Street and find a suitable parking space, but do **not** use the pub car parks without the landlord's permission.

Notes: Heavy nettle growth may be encountered on path KW38 in the summer months.

Great Offley, on the old Hitchin–Luton road at the top of the Chiltern escarpment, was formerly an important stopping point for travellers whose horses or legs were weary from the steep climb. Even today, although the A505 now bypasses the village, it is still characterised by its old coaching inns. Its location also makes it an ideal centre for walking as not only does Great Offley give access to the escarpment with its steep slopes and spectacular views (explored by Walks 26 and 28), but, in addition, it offers walks in the quiet and beautiful Chiltern uplands around Lilley Bottom and Kings Walden. It is therefore hardly surprising that two leading twentieth-century walkers, Don Gresswell MBE, for more than 50 years active in walking and path protection groups and founder of the Chiltern Society's Rights of Way Group, and Ron Pigram, well-known author of London Transport and other walks books, chose to live here. The village also has a long history being named after King Offa II of Mercia, who is believed to have had a palace here and died here in 796. In the eighteenth century it was home to Sir Thomas Salusbury, Judge of the High Court of Admiralty, who rebuilt his home of Offley Place and the chancel of the parish church (see Walk 28) where monuments to himself and other family members are housed. His niece, Hester Thrale, who often stayed at Offley

Place as a child, also came to prominence as a friend of Dr Johnson.

The walk explores the quiet upland countryside to the south of Great Offley, crossing Lilley Bottom to the hilltop hamlets of Mangrove Green, Cockernhoe and Tea Green before returning by a parallel route and abounds with extensive views of the surrounding hills.

Starting from the crossroads near the 'Green Man', take the Luton road, soon passing the 'Prince Henry'. At a right-hand bend, fork left onto a side-road, ignoring Salusbury Lane to your left and taking a narrow road straight on out of the village. After a quarter mile just before a cottage where the right-hand hedge ends permitting a fine view ahead towards Lilley, turn left onto path OF11, a grassy track left of the cottage, and follow it beside a left-hand hedge through two fields with wide views across Lilley Bottom to your right. Near the far end of the second field, ignore a branching track to your left and take path OF13 straight on beside a left-hand hedge. Soon, where the hedge and track bear right, continue to follow them past Westbury Wood through two fields and a belt of trees. Where the track turns left, leave it and go straight on, heading for an isolated house in Lilley Bottom to reach a hedge gap by a wooden pylon. Go through this gap and continue straight on to reach a road in front of the house.

Turn left onto this road, then, at the corner of the garden hedge, turn right onto path OF44 following a rough track straight on climbing gently for over three-quarters of a mile until you reach a gate near Mangrove Hall where the track turns left. Here turn right through another gate and follow the left-hand fence to a set of gates in the corner of the field. Turn left through these gates onto path OF50, following a left-hand hedge bearing left to reach a gate. Go through this and follow a fenced track straight on past Mangrove Hall to reach the end of a road by the 'King William IV' at Mangrove Green.

The twin hilltop hamlets of Mangrove Green and Cockernhoe with their greens and scattered cottages give a deceptively rural impression which belies the fact that both are now less than half a mile from the edge of Luton with its voracious appetite for building land. It is largely the existence of the county boundary which they have to thank for so far being spared the fate of nearby Stopsley which has long been swamped by urban development.

Take the road straight on across the green, then, after it becomes enclosed, at a right-hand bend, fork left onto fenced path OF25, which leads you between a hedge and a fence to a stile into a field. Bear slightly right across the field to cross another stile. Now follow a left-hand hedge straight on to a stile into a fenced path which leads you out to a road at Cockernhoe Green. Turn left onto this road, then at a junction, turn right onto a road towards Tea Green and Wandon End. Follow this winding road for a quarter mile, then, on entering Brickkiln Wood, turn right over a stile by a gate onto path OF3 and follow its obvious course flanked by hazel bushes through the wood. When you emerge from the wood, follow its outside edge, then a left-hand hedge straight on with Luton Airport and the outskirts of the town coming into view to your right. Where the hedge ends, bear slightly right across the field to the corner of a sporadic hedge, then bear half left and follow the hedge to the corner of a garden hedge at Crouchmoor Farm. Here follow this hedge straight on to a gate leading to a road junction, then turn left onto the road into Tea Green.

On reaching the green, keep right at a fork passing the 'White Horse' and continuing out of the hamlet. After a quarter mile, soon after the beginning of a left-hand hedge, turn left through a bollarded hedge gap onto path OF23 following what is usually a crop break uphill, turning right then left to reach a corner of Stubbocks Wood. Here turn right and follow its outside edge with fine views of Lilley Bottom, later passing through a hedge gap and descending into the valley. At the bottom corner of the wood, leave it and go straight on heading for the near right-hand corner of Furzen Wood to reach a hedge gap leading to a road.

Cross the road and take path KW38 straight on through a hedge gap, following the outside edge of Furzen Wood uphill. At a corner of the field, bear slightly left to enter the wood and take an ill-defined path straight on through it to emerge into a green lane. Turn left into this lane, ignoring a branching track to your right and later emerging into a field. At the far end of the wood, take a grassy track turning right and climbing to reach a hedge at the top of the field. Here, where the track turns left, leave it and go straight on through a hedge gap, then bear half left across the corner of a field to the near corner of Judkin's Wood. Now bear half right onto a grassy track along the outside edge of the wood. At the next corner of the wood, turn left onto path KW39 still following its outside edge. Where the edge of the wood turns left again, leave it and bear slightly right across a field to a hedge gap by the corner of a wood called Woodfern Wick. Here ignore a crossing track, go straight on through a gap and follow the outside edge of the wood, then, at a corner of the wood, bear half right across a field to a corner of Angel's Wood. Now take path OF24 along its outside edge to pass through a hedge gap, then bear half right onto path OF12 crossing a field diagonally, heading for a group of buildings around Great Offley House to reach a stile left of double gates in the far corner of the field. Cross this and follow the outside edge of a copse straight on to a further stile, then go straight on across the next field,

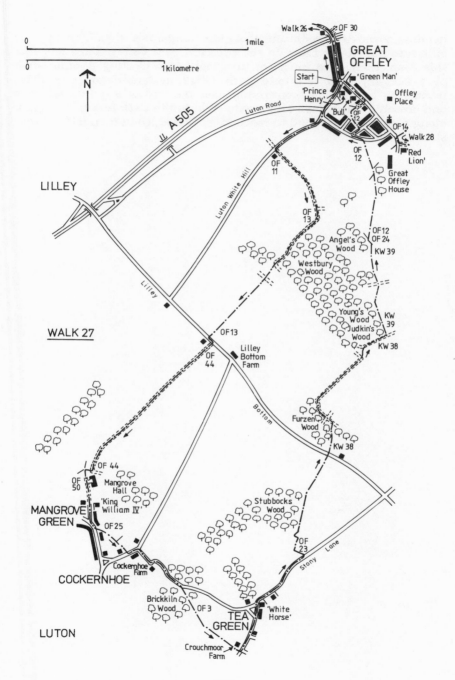

0 —————————————— 1mile
0 —————————————— 1kilometre
N

Walk 26 ← OF 30
GREAT OFFLEY
'Green Man'
Start
'Prince Henry'
Offley Place
'Bull'
OF 12
OF 14
Walk 28
OF 12
'Red Lion'
Luton Road
A 505
OF 11
Great Offley House
LILLEY
Luton White Hill
OF 13
OF 12 OF 24
KW 39
Angel's Wood
Westbury Wood
Lilley
Young's Wood
KW 39
Judkin's Wood
KW 38
WALK 27
OF 13
OF 44
Lilley Bottom Farm
Bottom
Furzen Wood
KW 38
OF 44
OF 50
Mangrove Hall
MANGROVE GREEN
'King William IV'
Stubbocks Wood
OF 25
OF 23
Stony Lane
Cockernhoe Farm
COCKERNHOE
Brickkiln Wood
OF 3
TEA GREEN
'White Horse'
LUTON
Crouchmoor Farm

145

heading towards a radio mast behind bungalows ahead, to reach a stile into Salusbury Lane on the edge of Great Offley. Turn left onto this road, then, at a junction, turn right into Gosling Avenue. Just past No. 48, turn left onto path OF12, a fenced concrete drive narrowing by garages, continuing past the end of a cul-de-sac road and crossing the village allotments. Where the path forks, bear right along a stony access road to reach High Street, then turn left for your starting point.

WALK 28: Hitchin

Length of Walk: 7.4 miles / 11.9 Km

Starting Point: Entrance to car park in Old Charlton Road, Hitchin.

Grid Ref: TL182289

Maps: OS Landranger Sheet 166
OS Pathfinder Sheet TL02/12

How to get there / Parking: From the Hitchin Hill roundabout at the junction of the A602 and B656, take the B656 towards the town centre. At the next mini-roundabout, turn left into Bridge Street, then after about 300 yards, turn left again into Old Charlton Road, where there is a long-stay car park on your left.

Hitchin, on the River Hiz, a tributary of the Ivel and Great Ouse, at the north-eastern extremity of the Chilterns, is probably the most beautiful town in the whole Chiltern area. Already settled in the Bronze Age, Hitchin and its river only derived their names in the Anglo-Saxon period when the town became the home of the Hicce tribe. It was, however, in the Middle Ages that the town became rich as a centre of the wood trade which supplied the Flanders weavers. This can be seen in St. Mary's Church, a thirteenth-century building lavishly remodelled by rich wool merchants in the fifteenth century. Amongst its many treasures, this massive church contains numerous brasses and a fifteenth-century font with a beautiful carved spire-shaped canopy. Apart from its church, the town, the centre of which retains its mediaeval street pattern, can boast a wealth of picturesque buildings including half-timbered houses with overhangs dating back to the fifteenth and sixteenth centuries and therefore is well worth exploring before or after your walk.

The walk soon leaves the town behind and leads you southwestwards past the hamlets of Charlton, birthplace in 1813 of Sir Henry Bessemer, inventor of an improved steel-making process, and Wellhead at the source of the River Hiz and across the Chiltern foothills with wide views of the escarpment before climbing the escarpment to Great Offley. You then turn southeastwards across the hilltop plateau to

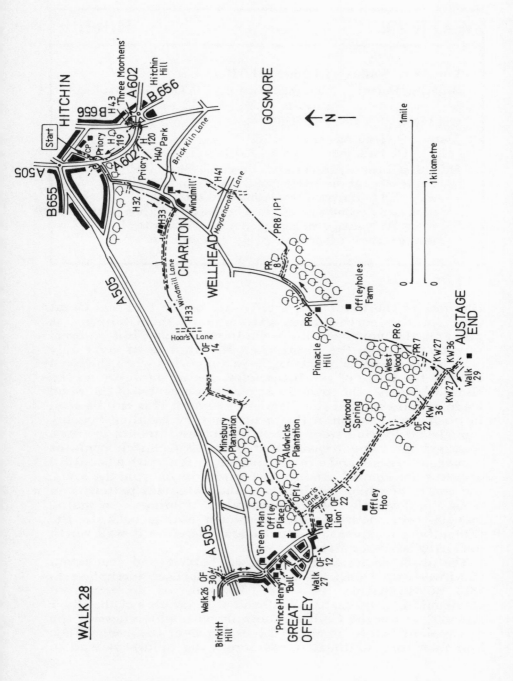

WALK 28

near Austage End before descending into a peaceful combe near Offleyholes Farm, crossing further foothills with extensive views and returning into Hitchin.

Starting from the entrance to the car park in Old Charlton Road, Hitchin, turn left onto this road and follow it to its end. Here turn right between anti-cycle barriers onto path H119, passing through an underpass, then turning left onto a macadam path which leads you to the junction of the A602 and Charlton Road. Now turn right into Charlton Road, soon crossing to its left-hand pavement. After some 200 yards at the second road junction, turn left (still on Charlton Road). At a slight left-hand bend, turn right through a white gate, then immediately left onto path H32 heading for the right-hand end of a group of trees right of a cottage, to cross a rail stile by a wooden shed. Now follow a left-hand fence straight on. Where the fence turns left, leave it and go straight on across a field to a hedge gap right of a group of cottages where a stile leads you out to a road at Charlton.

Do not join this road, but instead turn right onto bridleway H33, a rough sunken lane called Windmill Lane, and follow this gently uphill, soon with wide views of the hills to your left. Just past a cottage, where the rough road ends, go straight on through a gap by a gate into a wide green lane and follow it for a third of a mile. Where the lane opens into a field, follow the right-hand hedge straight on to its end then go straight on across a field to a hedge gap by a storm-damaged beech tree.

Here cross an old green lane called Hoars Lane and take bridleway OF14 straight on through the hedge gap and beside a left-hand hedge for nearly half a mile. On reaching a bend in a green lane by a wooden electricity pylon, turn left into it. After nearly a quarter mile where the lane turns left, leave it, turning right onto path OF14 and following a left-hand hedge. Where the hedge turns left, continue to follow it, eventually crossing a stile by the corner of a wood called Minsbury Plantation. Now follow the outside edge of the wood straight on. At the far side of the wood, turn right through a hedge gap and bear half left across the corner of a field to the corner of a fenced plantation. Now follow the plantation fence, later the outside edge of a mature wood, straight on uphill. At the top corner of the field, there is a fine view behind you across Hitchin and the lowlands to the north. Having admired this view, bear left onto a track into the wood. On leaving the wood, follow its outside edge straight on with views across the hills to your left. At the far end of the field, go straight on through a hedge gap and take a fenced path along the edge of the wood and past the churchyard to a stile onto Great Offley village street near the church and the 'Red Lion'.

The church to your right dates from the thirteenth century, but its chancel was rebuilt in about 1750 by Sir Thomas Salusbury of nearby Offley Place, a judge of the High Court of Admiralty, to display his family monuments, while the tower was rebuilt in brick in 1814. Inside are a beautiful fourteenth-century font and eighteenth-century monuments by Sir Robert Taylor and Nollekens.

Turn left onto this road, then by the 'Red Lion', fork left into a rough lane called Harris Lane. After some 350 yards at a sharp left-hand bend, leave the lane and take bridleway OF22 straight on following a grassy track beside a right-hand hedge. At the far side of the field at two track junctions, go straight on, taking a rough track across a large field to pass through a hedge gap at the corner of a wood called Cockrood Spring. Now bear half right, leaving the track and crossing a field diagonally to a hedge gap in the far corner where you rejoin the track. Go through this gap and keep to the track, turning left and following a left-hand hedge, later the outside edge of West Wood (now on KW36).

At the far end of the field ignore a branching track into the wood and go straight on through a hedge gap. Now take the track straight on through two more fields. At the far end of the second field, where you briefly meet the route of Walk 29, turn left through a hedge gap onto path KW27, following a right-hand hedge to the far side of the field. Here turn right through a hedge gap then immediately left through a second and cross a track by a left-hand gate. Now take path PR7 (later joining bridleway PR6) following the outside edge of West Wood straight on, eventually starting to descend the escarpment. On nearing the bottom corner of the field, the bridleway bears left and drops through a corner of the wood to reach a gate in the valley bottom. Go through this and follow a right-hand hedge straight on along the valley bottom to a gate into a copse. Take the obvious path straight on through the copse to a bridlegate, then follow a right-hand iron parkland fence straight on. Where the iron railings end, go straight on across the field to a gate leading to a bend in a road.

Take this road straight on for nearly a quarter mile passing a copse to your left. At a left-hand bend by the corner of a wood on a hillside to your right, turn right onto bridleway PR8 taking a track uphill to the corner of the wood. Here go straight on along the edge of the wood, through an outcrop of woodland, then beside a right-hand fence. Where the grassy track ends, bear half left across a corner of a field to the corner of a hedge, then take bridleway PR8/IP1 bearing half left to follow a right-hand hedge over the brow of a hill with wide views to your left at first. After nearly half a mile at a corner of the field, go straight on through a hedge gap into an ancient sunken lane called Tatmorehills Lane and turn left into it, soon reaching Maydencroft Lane.

Cross this road and take bridleway H41 straight on through a hedge gap, following a right-hand hedge, which bears left at one point, to reach a hedge gap at the far end of the field. Go through this and turn left to reach Brick Kiln Lane, then cross this road and go through a fence gap opposite into Priory Park. Now bear half right onto path H40 heading between Hitchin Priory, a Palladian eighteenth-century mansion incorporating parts of a fourteenth-century Carmelite priory, and a clump of trees, to reach a signpost by the fence of the A602. Here turn right onto path H120 following the A602 fence to a kissing-gate leading to a footbridge. Turn left over this footbridge, then at its far end, turn left through a gap in the railings onto path H43 following a left-hand fence through a copse. On reaching a kissing-gate, turn left onto fenced path H119, soon meeting and following the A602 fence. Where the path widens out, follow the right-hand fence, soon passing through a plantation to join the A602 at the River Hiz bridge. Cross this bridge, then fork right onto fenced path H119 which soon leads you to the end of Old Charlton Road where your starting point is straight ahead.

WALK 29: Preston

Length of Walk: 7.3 miles / 11.7 Km

Starting Point: 'Red Lion', Preston.

Grid Ref: TL180247

Maps: OS Landranger Sheet 166
OS Pathfinder Sheet TL02/12

How to get there / Parking: Preston, some 2.5 miles south of Hitchin, may be reached from the Hitchin Hill roundabout at the junction of the A602 and B656 by taking the road signposted to Gosmore for 2.4 miles, passing through Gosmore and continuing straight on to Preston. At the village green, find a suitable parking space in the side roads around it, but do **not** use the pub car park without the landlord's permission.

Notes: Heavy nettle growth may be encountered in summer, particularly on paths KW49 and KW34.

Preston, with its leafy green, with an attractive well and pub, is the epitome of the English village. Like most villages, it has a long history, its manor of 'Deneslai' being listed in the Domesday Book. In 1147 the manor was given to the Knights Templar, an order of warrior-monks, who held it till their suppression in 1312, and thus it became known as Temple Dinsley. The manor was subsequently held by another monastic order called the Knights Hospitaller before it fell to the Crown in the reformation. The present house, built in 1714 and greatly enlarged by Sir Edwin Lutyens in 1908, is now a private girls' school. The vicinity of Preston, however, also has other religious associations, as nearby Wain Wood was the scene of secret midnight services with massive congregations held by the Puritan writer and preacher John Bunyan, author of 'Pilgrim's Progress', while modern Castle Farm stands on the site of Hunsdon House whose non-conformist occupants also suffered seventeenth-century religious persecution. This same house was converted in the 1760s to resemble a castle (hence the name of the farm) by Captain Robert Hinde, an eccentric retired army officer, whom the contemporary author, Laurence Sterne took as the model for his Uncle Toby in his 'Tristram Shandy'.

The walk leads you from Preston through the quiet, rolling hill country around King's Walden to the west, crossing Lilley Bottom to the hilltop village of Breachwood Green, before returning by a parallel route.

Starting from the 'Red Lion' at Preston, take the Hitchin road. After about 120 yards, fork left into Chequers Lane. On passing a row of cottages called Chequers Cottages, turn left through a small gate onto path PR4 passing between hedges to enter a field. Now follow its right-hand hedge straight on. At the far side of the field, go through a hedge gap and continue between a hedge and a line of fence posts to reach Butcher's Lane. Turn left onto this road and after about 35 yards, turn right over a concealed stile onto path PR5. Now bear slightly right across a field, passing right of a black wooden cowshed to reach two large holly bushes. Here bear half left following a sporadic line of trees to a gate, then go straight on across the next field to a stile left of double gates leading into Dead Woman's Lane (KW48), part of an ancient road from Hitchin to Kimpton.

Turn right into this green lane and follow it for some 350 yards. Where its left-hand hedge ends, turn left, ignoring a track to your left, and take path KW37 across a field heading just right of a black barn with a red-tiled roof at Austage End, to reach a sunken green lane by two holly trees. Turn left into this lane (KW46) and after about 120 yards, by a tall oak tree, turn right onto path KW 37 crossing a field to the left-hand end of a line of oaks. Here go straight on through newly-planted trees to pass right of a lightning-damaged oak tree and a telegraph pole, then follow a left-hand hedge passing left of a large new house to reach a road at Austage End.

Turn left onto this road and after about 50 yards at a left-hand bend, turn right onto a grassy track (KW36), passing through a hedge gap and bearing right to follow a right-hand hedge. At the far side of the field, follow the track wiggling to the right through a hedge gap to meet the route of Walk 28, then turn left onto path KW27 following a left-hand hedge. Where the hedge turns right, go straight on through a hedge gap and across the corner of a field to a hedge gap by the left-hand of two oak trees. Now go straight on across the next field to a hedge gap leading into a green lane. Turn right into this lane, immediately bearing left and descending to reach Stopsley Holes Farm.

Here take a track straight on between the farm buildings to the end of a road. Now follow this road straight on uphill for some 300 yards ignoring a branching road to the left. Just after a right-hand bend shaded by overhanging trees, turn left onto path KW25, a grassy track leading up into a field. On reaching the edge of the field, turn sharp right through bushes onto path KW49 to cross a stile by a bridlegate.

Now follow this hedged path straight on for some 250 yards, crossing two more stiles and eventually reaching a road. Turn left onto this road and after some 60 yards, before reaching a powerline, turn right through a hedge gap onto path KW12 bearing slightly left across a field, with wide views of Lilley Bottom opening out ahead, to reach the corner of a hedge at the left-hand end of a line of oaks. Now bear half right across the next field to the corner of a hedge. Here go through a hedge gap and follow a right-hand hedge downhill. At the bottom end of the field, follow the hedge turning right, then, at a corner, go straight on through the hedge into the next field. Now turn left and follow the left-hand hedge downhill to the road in Lilley Bottom.

Cross this road bearing slightly left and take path KW33 following a left-hand hedge gently uphill. After some 200 yards, where the hedge turns left, follow it to a corner of the field, then turn right and follow the winding left-hand hedge, later a crop break. Where the crop break widens into an area of scrub, keep left of the scrub and follow its outside edge uphill with fine views of Lilley Bottom to your left and the ruins of Darleyhall Windmill soon coming into view ahead. At the top corner of the field, go straight on into a green lane and follow it to the end of a road at The Heath, a hamlet on the edge of Breachwood Green.

Continue along this road, ignoring a branching road to the right, then, at a T-junction, take the major road straight on over a crossroads towards Breachwood Green, another village connected with John Bunyan as the pulpit he used when preaching at nearby Bendish in 1658 is housed in the village's ninety-year-old Baptist chapel. After the right-hand houses end, at a right-hand bend by the village allotments, turn left through a hedge gap onto path KW14, following this obvious path to the end of a hedge. Here bear slightly right and later bear slightly left to reach a stile into Lord's Wood. Follow the obvious path straight on through the wood, then at its far side, ignore a branching path to the right and follow the outside edge of the wood, later a left-hand hedge, straight on downhill to the road in Lilley Bottom.

Cross this road and a stile opposite, then bear slightly right uphill to cross stiles in two fences. Here go straight on to cross a stile in a clump of trees right of the top corner of the field leading into Garden Wood. In the wood turn left onto path KW19 which soon emerges over a stile into a field. Here turn right and follow the outside edge of the wood, then where it turns right by a tall oak, leave it and go straight on downhill and up again with glimpses of Kingswalden Bury, rebuilt in neo-Georgian style in 1972 to replace a Victorian predecessor, through the trees to your right, to reach a gate onto King's Walden village street.

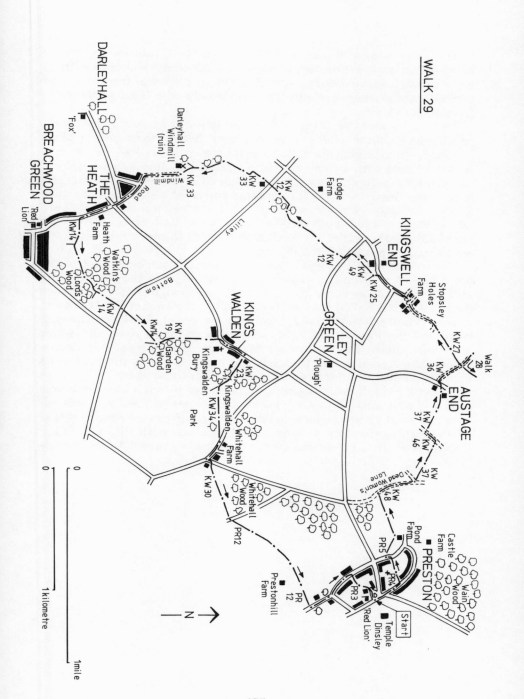

The name King's Walden is derived from the village having been a royal manor in a wooded area. Its thirteenth-century church with its notable fourteenth-century painted screen and a tower from the same period contains memorials to the Hale family who lived at the Bury from 1595 to 1885.

Turn right onto the village street and follow it for nearly 300 yards passing the church and a large red-brick house, then near a black cowshed, turn right through gates onto path KW23 crossing a parkland field with a clear view of Kingswalden Bury to your right at one point, heading somewhat left of a tall cedar to reach a kissing-gate onto a tree-lined drive. Go through this and cross a stile opposite, then follow a left-hand fence straight on until you reach a stile in it. Turn left over this onto path KW34, then bear half right across the parkland passing right of two clumps of trees to reach a kissing-gate onto a road opposite Whitehall House.

Turn right onto this road, soon ignoring a branching road to the left, then at a second road junction, turn left onto the Preston and Hitchin road. After some 70 yards, just past a right-hand barn, turn right onto path KW30 into the farmyard. At the rear of the farmyard, bear half left across the field, heading for a group of oaks on the next ridge, eventually descending a steep bank to join a road. Cross this and take path PR12 through a hedge gap virtually opposite, descending a steep bank, then bearing half left across the field to its far left-hand corner. Here go through the left-hand of two hedge gaps and bear right following the right-hand hedge through four fields to a gate and stile leading to a road on the outskirts of Preston. Turn left onto this road, then at a fork go left. Just past Preston Primary School on the right, turn right onto enclosed macadam path PR3 and follow this through to a cul-de-sac lane which leads you out to the village green near the 'Red Lion'.

WALK 30:   St. Paul's Walden

Length of Walk: (A) 7.2 miles / 11.5 Km
                       (B) 2.5 miles / 4.0 Km
                       (C) 5.2 miles / 8.3 Km

Starting Point: Southern entrance gates to St. Paul's
                       Walden churchyard.

Grid Ref: TL193222

Maps: OS Landranger Sheet 166
           OS Pathfinder Sheet TL02/12

How to get there / Parking: St. Paul's Walden, some 4.3
   miles south of Hitchin, may be reached from the town by
   taking the B656 towards Codicote for about 2.5 miles,
   then turning right onto the B651 towards Whitwell. After
   some 1.8 miles, at a crossroads by the 'Strathmore Arms',
   turn right onto a road signposted to St. Paul's Walden
   Church and park by the church avoiding blocking field
   entrances. In case of difficulty, Walks A and B can also be
   started from Whitwell, where on-street parking is possible
   in places.

Notes: Heavy nettle growth may be encountered in summer on
   Walks A and C, particularly on path PW12 and bridleway
   LA17.

St. Paul's Walden, set in hillside parkland above the Mimram
valley in the far north-east corner of the Chilterns, is probably
best known as the birthplace in 1900 of Queen Elizabeth the
Queen Mother, daughter of the Earl of Strathmore, whose
family, the Bowes-Lyons (formerly Bowes), have owned St.
Paul's Waldenbury for more than 200 years. The present
house, which can be seen from Walks A and B, was built in
1767 and considerably extended in 1887. The parish church,
where the Queen Mother was christened and which she
attended as a child, dates from the fourteenth century and has
a chancel rebuilt by Edward Gilbert in 1727. When this church
was built, however, the village had another name as it was
then called Abbot's Walden because the manor belonged to St.
Alban's Abbey, but during the reformation, the manor passed
to St. Paul's Cathedral and so was renamed St. Paul's Walden
in 1544. The royal wedding in 1923 did not, however, create the

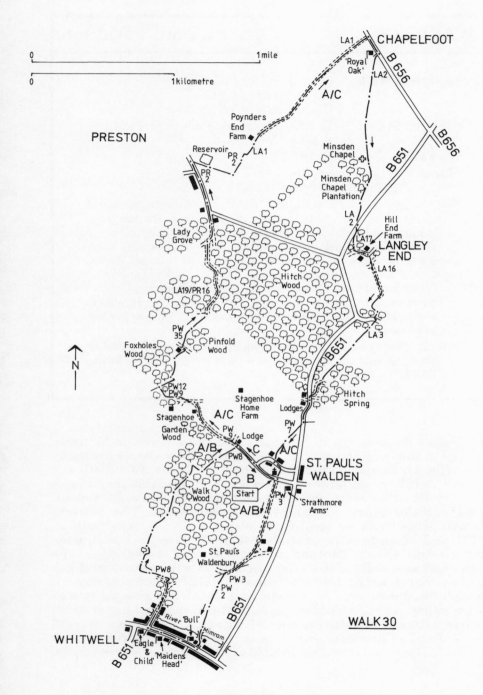

CHAPELFOOT

LA1

'Royal Oak'

LA2

B 656

B 656

A/C

PRESTON

Poynders End Farm

Minsden Chapel

Reservoir

PR 2   LA1

PR 2

Minsden Chapel Plantation

B 651

LA 2

Lady Grove

Hill End Farm

LA17

LANGLEY END

LA 16

Hitch Wood

LA19/PR16

LA 2

LA 3

PW 35

B 651

Foxholes Wood

Pinfold Wood

PW12 PW9

Hitch Spring

Stagenhoe Home Farm

A/C

Lodges

Stagenhoe Garden Wood

PW 9   Lodge

PW 7

A/B

PW8

C

A/C

ST. PAUL'S WALDEN

B

Start

Walk Wood

PW 3

'Strathmore Arms'

A/B

PW8

St. Paul's Waldenbury

PW 3

PW 2

B 651

WHITWELL

River 'Bull'

Mimram

WALK 30

B 651

Eagle & Child'

'Maidens Head'

N

0 ——————————— 1 mile

0 ——————————— 1 kilometre

158

village's first royal connection, as there is a memorial in the church to Henry Stapleford who died in 1631, having acted as servant to three very different monarchs, Elizabeth I, James I and Charles I.

Walks A and B lead you southwards from the village through attractive parkland with fine views, to the olde worlde village of Whitwell in the picturesque Mimram valley, while Walks A and C explore the wooded hills to the north dropping to Chapelfoot in the Ippollitts valley before returning by way of the ruins of Minsden Chapel and the hamlet of Langley End to St. Paul's Walden.

Starting from the southern entrance gates to St. Paul's Walden churchyard, **Walk C** turns right along the road and follows it straight on for a quarter mile to where its macadam surface ends by a lodge. Now take its stony continuation, path PW9, straight on and omit the next two paragraphs.

Walks A and B also start from these gates, but cross the road and take path PW3, a fenced track, straight on descending gently for a quarter mile through old parkland. By a cottage called 'The Garden House', take a macadam drive straight on, ignoring a branching drive to the left and continuing uphill to cross an avenue of trees where you can obtain a view of St. Paul's Waldenbury to your right. On rounding a right-hand bend, fork left through a kissing-gate by a field gate onto path PW2 and bear half left, following a line of trees across a parkland field to a kissing-gate left of a gate where a view of Whitwell (pronounced 'Whittle') in the Mimram valley opens out ahead. Now follow a right-hand fence downhill to a gate and stile leading to a footbridge over the River Mimram (until recent years often given the alternative name of Maran). Cross this bridge and bear slightly left across a field to a gate and stile, then follow a rough drive bearing right to reach the B651, Whitwell High Street, with its ancient inns and cottages.

Turn right onto this road and follow it through the village, then, by the 'Eagle and Child' (which, though enlarged in 1747, may date from the sixteenth century as its name refers to the crest of the Stanley family who lived at Stagenhoe in the early sixteenth century) and a half-timbered cottage called The Tannery, turn right into a cul-de-sac road known as The Valley, soon recrossing the Mimram. Where its macadam surface ends, take its stony continuation straight on up a deep tree-lined sunken lane. Where the lane forks, turn left onto path PW8 to reach a gate into a field. Do not go through this gate, but turn right through a kissing-gate into another field, then turn left and follow a left-hand hedge. At the far end of the field, turn right and follow a left-hand hedge uphill. At the next corner, turn right again and after a few yards, turn left through a kissing-gate. Now follow the left-hand hedge straight on through two fields to a kissing-gate into Walk Wood. In this wood follow a winding path straight on, soon passing a field to your left. About 150 yards beyond the far side of the field the path turns sharp right, then 100 yards further on, it turns sharp left. Eventually a field comes into view to your left and you soon emerge into another field. Here follow the left-hand hedge straight on to reach the end of a macadam road by an old lodge of Stagenhoe Park where **Walk B** turns right onto the road and follows it straight on back to your starting point, while **Walk A** turns left onto the road's stony continuation (path PW9).

Walks A and C now follow the track's winding course past Garden Wood and an unusual Jacobean cottage to reach the macadam drive to Stagenhoe Park. Mentioned in the Domesday Book, its present house was built in 1737 and is now a Sue Ryder Home. In the 1880s it was occupied by Sir Arthur Sullivan, who composed 'The Mikado' here and outraged local people by his life-style. Turn left onto the drive (still path PW9) with views of the house to your left. Where the drive forks by a white gate, fork right off it and follow a grassy path beside a left-hand fence straight on to a corner of the field. here go straight on through a hedge gap then turn right onto path PW12 through a second hedge gap to reach a barbed-wire fence. Now turn right onto a path into and through Foxholes Wood. On re-emerging into a field, turn left and follow the edge of the wood, then a garden fence to reach a farm road by a cottage.

Turn left onto the farm road passing the cottage. By some outbuildings, turn right onto path PW35 following the outside edge of Pinfold Wood. At a corner of the wood, leave it and bear half right across a field to a hedge gap into Hitch Wood. Here take path LA19/PR16, a wide winding track between mossy banks straddling the parish boundary between Langley and Preston, straight on for over a third of a mile, later with a field visible to your left. On reaching a T-junction with another track, turn right onto it and follow it to the end of a macadam road by some cottages. Now take this road straight on to a T-junction where you turn left soon passing the former Minsden Farm.

At a road junction take the Gosmore and Hitchin road straight on, then after about 70 yards, turn right through a hedge gap onto path PR2, following this narrow fenced path past an underground reservoir to a stile. Now follow a right-hand hedge straight on, turning left at a corner of the field and continuing until you reach a gap in the hedge. Here transfer to the other side of the hedge and take path LA1 still following the hedge to Poynders End Farm with its fine wooden barns and timber-framed farmhouse. Go straight on past the farm, then take a grassy track beside a left-hand hedge. Where the hedge turns left, follow the grassy track straight on with wide views across the valley towards Hitchin to your left and Stevenage beyond the next rise. Eventually the track joins a right-hand hedge which you follow to the B656 at Chapelfoot.

Turn right onto this road and follow it past the 'Royal Oak', part of which dates from the seventeenth century. At the far end of the pub garden, before reaching a black wooden barn, turn right onto bridleway LA2 passing the end of the pub and turning left by a wooden shed into a fenced path. On emerging into a field, follow the left-hand hedge straight on gently climbing. Where the hedge ends, keep straight on, heading just left of the ruins of Minsden Chapel to reach the corner of Minsden Chapel Plantation near the chapel ruins.

Built in the fourteenth century, Minsden Chapel was a chapel-of-ease of Hitchin parish serving the lost hamlet of 'Minlesden' referred to in the Domesday Book. By 1650 the hamlet would seem to have disappeared as the chapel was already reported to be in a decayed state and during the last recorded service at the chapel, a marriage in 1738, the curate is believed to have narrowly missed being struck by falling masonry. Earlier in the present century, the noted local historian, Reginald Hine, who was fascinated by these allegedly haunted ruins, leased them from the Church of England and was subsequently buried here in 1949.

Now follow the outside edge of the wood, later a right-hand hedge, straight on downhill. Where the hedge ends, take a winding grassy track straight on to a hedge gap leading to the B651. Turn right onto this road, then fork immediately left onto bridleway LA17 which climbs gently through hillside scrubland. On reaching a grassy track, turn left onto it to reach the end of a macadam road by Hill End Farm at Langley End. Take this road straight on, then at a left-hand bend, fork right onto path LA16 passing through a copse to cross a stile. Now take a fenced track beside a right-hand hedge straight on, ignoring a branching track to the right. At the far end of the field, bear right between hedges to cross a stile into a hedged path. Follow its winding course to a narrow road, then turn left onto the road and immediately right over a stile onto path LA3 heading for the right-hand end of a coniferous plantation to cross a stile. Now go straight on, at first skirting the conifers, then striking out through bracken to join a track straight on through a copse called Hitch Spring to reach the B651.

Turn left onto this road passing the lodge gates of Stagenhoe Park surmounted by stags and wrought-ironwork, then on rounding a left-hand bend, turn right through a hedge gap onto path PW7, bearing left across a field keeping left of a line of three trees to reach the corner of a hedge. Here follow the left-hand hedge straight on and on nearing a cottage, bear slightly left onto a path between a hedge and a fence leading to a narrow road at St. Paul's Walden. Turn left onto this road passing the White House, then at a left-hand bend, fork right onto path PW3 passing through the churchyard to reach your starting point.

Index of Place Names

Books Published by
THE BOOK CASTLE

CHANGES IN OUR LANDSCAPE: ASPECTS OF BEDFORDSHIRE, BUCKINGHAMSHIRE and the CHILTERNS, 1947–1992: from the photographic work of Eric Meadows. 350+ fascinating colour and monochrome pictures by the area's leading landscape photographer. Detailed introduction and captions.

JOURNEYS INTO HERTFORDSHIRE: Anthony Mackay. Foreword by The Marquess of Salisbury, Hatfield House. Nearly 200 superbly detailed ink drawings depict the towns, buildings and landscape of this still predominantly rural county.

JOURNEYS INTO BEDFORDSHIRE: Anthony Mackay. Foreword by The Marquess of Tavistock, Woburn Abbey. A lavish book of over 150 evocative ink drawings.

NORTH CHILTERNS CAMERA, 1863–1954: FROM THE THURSTON COLLECTION IN LUTON MUSEUM: edited by Stephen Bunker. Rural landscapes, town views, studio pictures and unique royal portraits by the area's leading early photographer.

THE CHANGING FACE OF LUTON: A PICTORIAL HISTORY: Stephen Bunker, Robin Holgate and Marian Nichols. Well-illustrated account from earliest times to the present-day by the expert staff of Luton Museum.

LEAFING THROUGH LITERATURE: WRITERS' LIVES IN HERTFORDSHIRE AND BEDFORDSHIRE: David Carroll. Illustrated short biographies of many famous authors and their connections with these counties.

THROUGH VISITORS' EYES: A BEDFORDSHIRE ANTHOLOGY: edited by Simon Houfe. Impressions of the county by famous visitors over the last four centuries, thematically arranged and illustrated with line drawings.

THE HILL OF THE MARTYR: AN ARCHITECTURAL HISTORY OF ST. ALBANS ABBEY: Eileen Roberts. Scholarly and readable chronological narrative history of Hertfordshire and Bedfordshire's famous cathedral. Fully illustrated with photographs and plans.

ECHOES: TALES and LEGENDS of BEDFORDSHIRE and HERTFORDSHIRE: Vic Lea. Thirty, compulsively retold historical incidents.

LOCAL WALKS: SOUTH BEDFORDSHIRE and NORTH CHILTERNS: Vaughan Basham. Twenty-seven thematic circular walks.

CHILTERN WALKS: BUCKINGHAMSHIRE: Nick Moon. In association with the Chiltern Society, one of a series of three guides to the whole Chilterns. Thirty circular walks.

CHILTERN WALKS: OXFORDSHIRE and WEST BUCKINGHAMSHIRE: Nick Moon. In association with the Chiltern Society, another book of thirty circular walks.

CHILTERN WALKS: HERTFORDSHIRE, BEDFORDSHIRE and NORTH BUCKINGHAMSHIRE: Nick Moon. Completes the trilogy of circular walks, in association with the Chiltern Society.

COUNTRY AIR: SUMMER and AUTUMN: Ron Wilson. The Radio Northampton presenter looks month by month at the countryside's wildlife, customs and lore.

COUNTRY AIR: WINTER and SPRING: Ron Wilson. This companion volume completes the year in the countryside.

WHIPSNADE WILD ANIMAL PARK: 'MY AFRICA': Lucy Pendar. Foreword by Andrew Forbes. Introduction by Gerald Durrell. Inside story of sixty years of the Park's animals and people – full of anecdotes, photographs and drawings.

FARM OF MY CHILDHOOD, 1925–1947: Mary Roberts. An almost vanished lifestyle on a remote farm near Flitwick.

SWANS IN MY KITCHEN: The Story of a Swan Sanctuary: Lis Dorer. Foreword by Dr Philip Burton. Tales of her dedication to the survival of these beautiful birds through her sanctuary near Hemel Hempstead.

A LASTING IMPRESSION: Michael Dundrow. An East End boy's wartime experiences as an evacuee on a Chilterns farm at Totternhoe.

EVA'S STORY: CHESHAM SINCE the TURN of the CENTURY: Eva Rance. The ever-changing twentieth-century, especially the early years at her parents' general stores, Tebby's, in the High Street.

DUNSTABLE DECADE: THE EIGHTIES: – A Collection of Photographs: Pat Lovering. A souvenir book of nearly 300 pictures of people and events in the 1980s.

DUNSTABLE IN DETAIL: Nigel Benson. A hundred of the town's buildings and features, plus town trail map.

OLD DUNSTABLE: Bill Twaddle. A new edition of this collection of early photographs.

BOURNE AND BRED: A DUNSTABLE BOYHOOD BETWEEN THE WARS: Colin Bourne. An elegantly written, well-illustrated book capturing the spirit of the town over fifty years ago.

ROYAL HOUGHTON: Pat Lovering. Illustrated history of Houghton Regis from the earliest times to the present.

Specially for Children

ADVENTURE ON THE KNOLLS: A STORY OF IRON AGE BRITAIN:
Michael Dundrow. Excitement on Totternhoe Knolls as ten-year-old John finds himself back in those dangerous times, confronting Julius Caesar and his army.

THE RAVENS: ONE BOY AGAINST THE MIGHT OF ROME:
James Dyer. On the Barton hills and in the south-east of England as the men of the great fort of Ravensburgh (near Hexton) confront the invaders.

Further titles are in preparation.
All the above are available via any bookshop, or from the publisher and bookseller

THE BOOK CASTLE
12 Church Street, Dunstable, Bedfordshire, LU5 4RU
Tel: (0582) 605670